TEACHING
DEUTERONOMY

Talk outlines for the book of Deuteronomy

CONTENTS

A. QUICK HELP: How to prepare a talk on Deuteronomy . . . 4

B. How to teach and preach 5

C. About the book of Deuteronomy 17

D. Study and teach Deuteronomy 19

E. How to apply Old Testament laws today 98

F. Lessons from Deuteronomy 100

Teaching Deuteronomy is published by The Good Book Company
© Paul Barker/The Good Book Company 2014

email: ppp@thegoodbook.co.uk

Websites
UK: www.thegoodbook.co.uk
North America: www.thegoodbook.com
Australia: www.thegoodbook.com.au
New Zealand: www.thegoodbook.co.nz

Unless indicated, all Scripture references are taken from the HOLY BIBLE, NEW INTERNATIONAL VERSION.
Copyright © 1973, 1978, 1984 International Bible Society. Used by permission.

ISBN: 9781908317322 • Printed in China.

The **Pray Prepare Preach** project is working in partnership with a growing number of organisations worldwide, including: Langham Partnership • Grace Baptist Mission • Pastor Training International (PTI) • Sovereign World Trust • Africa Inland Mission (AIM) • Worldshare • Entrust Foundation • India Bible Literature • African Pastors' Book Fund • Preacher's Help • African Christian Textbooks (ACTS) Nigeria • Orphans for Christ, Uganda • Project Timothy.

Also in this series:
Teaching God's Big Story • Preaching Mark • Preaching Philippians • Preaching Job • Teaching 2 Timothy

Please read this first!

It is a big joy to bring you another PPP book. We pray that this will help you to preach and teach God's word. We want people everywhere to hear God's word clearly. Then people will turn to Jesus. Christians will grow more like Jesus. God will have all the praise.

We give you a lot of help. But you must still work hard! Please do not just copy what you read!

PPP means Pray! Prepare! Preach! This book will help you to speak God's word if you are a preacher, or if you are a teacher of God's word in a school or church.

There is a lot to do before you preach or teach.

PRAY. We cannot change people's hearts. Only God can do that. We cannot make people believe. Only God can do that. We must pray before we prepare. Pray that you will hear God speak to you. We must pray before we speak. Pray that you will speak God's truth clearly. We must pray after we have taught God's word. Pray that your hearers respond to God's word.

PREPARE. It is hard work to prepare a Bible talk. It takes many hours. This book helps you, but it does not do all the work for you! You need to read the passage slowly. You need to study the verses carefully. You need to prepare what you will say to your hearers so that they will be helped.

PREACH. God works in wonderful ways when we teach his word! God's word is like seed that produces fruit in our lives—the fruit of the Spirit. It is an exciting thing to speak God's word. God has promised that his word will do his work.

Here is the best way to use this book. Read the "How to teach and preach" section. Then begin at the start of Deuteronomy. Teach each section in turn. It is a story. It makes most sense when you begin at the start and end at the end!

"All Scripture is God-breathed and is useful for teaching, rebuking, correcting and training in righteousness, so that the man of God may be thoroughly equipped for every good work" *2 Timothy 3:16-17.*

A. QUICK HELP:
How to prepare a talk on Deuteronomy

1. Pray for God's help.

▼

2. ☉ Read the Bible section several times.
Use ❂ **Background** and ❂ **Notes** to help you study the Bible verses.

▼

3. Try to find the main point that God is teaching us in the Bible section.
Use ⊕ **MAIN POINT** to help you.

▼

4. Pray for your people. Think how this Bible section will help them.
Use ☉ **Something to work on** to help you.

▼

5. Prepare your talk to give it in your own language. Make notes to help you. Keep to the main point.
Use our notes in the **TEACH** section to help you.

▼

6. Check what you have done.
- Is the **main point** clear?
- Do you show them what the **Bible** teaches?
- Do you use **word pictures** to help your people understand and remember?
- Do you **connect** with the people?
- What do you hope will **change**?

▼

7. Pray that God will speak through your words. Pray that his truth will change people.

For more help read the next section.

B: How to teach and preach

These pages explain how to teach the Bible. It will help to read them every time you prepare a new sermon or talk.

2 Timothy 2:15 says: "Work hard so you can present yourself to God and receive his approval. Be a good worker, one who does not need to be ashamed and who correctly explains the word of truth" (New Living Translation).

This verse is about teaching the Bible. Paul tells Timothy it is hard work. Many teachers and preachers only spend a few minutes preparing a message. That is not enough. It needs hard work. Imagine a man builds a wall. He is lazy. He does a bad job and the wall falls down. He will not be asked to build another one!

- *Why is it important to work hard at teaching the Bible?*
- *What will happen if we do not explain the Bible in the right way?*

If we do not explain the Bible, God will be sad. The people will not be helped.

If we do teach the Bible, people will be saved from hell. People will grow in the knowledge of Jesus and become more like Jesus.

Take as much time as you can to prepare a talk or sermon. Preparing a good talk or sermon may take a whole day! Remember to PRAY. Prayer is the first thing to do. Keep praying as you prepare, before you speak, and afterwards.

STUDY, TEACH

For each passage there are two parts:

STUDY—how to understand the passage

TEACH—how to give a sermon or talk from the passage

STUDY
Pray → Background → Read → Notes → Something to work on → Main point

TEACH
Start → 2 or 3 Sub-points → Illustration → Apply → Pray

STUDY

You will see the following headings in the Study section:

Background → Read → Notes → Something to work on → Main point

The Bible is God's word. When we teach the Bible, we must make sure people hear what God says. This means we must be very careful to find the **MAIN POINT** of a passage—because that is what God wants us to say!

When you know the **MAIN POINT**, you will know what God wants you to say. Then you can think how best to apply it to your hearers.

So how do you find the main point? Follow these steps:

1. Pray

Pray for God's help and **keep praying** as you prepare. We need the help of the Holy Spirit for our study and teaching to produce fruit.

2. Background

Think about the BACKGROUND to the passage.

What do we mean by BACKGROUND? Here is an illustration: Look at the first picture of a plane. What can you say about where the plane is?

Now look at this second picture at the top of the next page. It is the same picture, but now you can see the **background**. What can you say now about where the plane is?

You can see that the plane has landed. It is near a village. The sky is dark and it is a dangerous time to fly, so it must be an important journey.

The **background** makes a big difference to understanding. So, when we study God's word, we need to see the **background** to the passage.

This has three parts:

1. Where in the Bible the passage comes
2. Where in the book of the Bible the passage comes
3. What happens in the chapters or verses before and after the passage

When we know these things, we understand the Bible passage better.

Each talk will be from a few verses. These verses fit into the whole chapter, and the whole book and the whole Bible! Think how a passage builds on what was said before. For example, if you are speaking from Deuteronomy, to understand the background you need to think about:

The whole Bible

- Where in the Bible's story does this book come?
- Is it in the Old Testament (before Jesus came) or in the New Testament (when Jesus came)?
- When in the timeline of history is this book set? (The Bible tells the true story of the world.)
- References and footnotes may help us with how this passage fits into the whole Bible.

The whole book

- Who was Moses speaking to?
- Where were the people when Moses spoke to them?
- Why did Moses say these things to the people?

You may find help with background in the introduction in your Bible. You will find help in "About Deuteronomy" (p 17). For example, you will see that Moses was speaking to the people of Israel. They were on the edge of the promised land. Moses wanted to encourage the people to trust God and enter the promised land.

The passage before the one you will speak from

- Where is it in the book?
- What is the main point of the passage before this one?

For example, if you are preaching on Deuteronomy 2:1 – 3:11, you need to know what happened in 1:34-45, so that you understand why the people turned back from Kadesh Barnea (2:1).

3. Read

Read the Bible passage **three times**. Read it slowly and carefully. It is best to read out loud. Read it in a different translation if you have one. The third time, read it with your eyes and ears, your nose and hands! Imagine you were there. What will you see, hear, smell and feel?

4. Understand

Work on UNDERSTANDING the passage. To teach a passage well, you need to understand clearly what it says.

Look carefully at this picture of the plane. What can you learn about what IS happening?

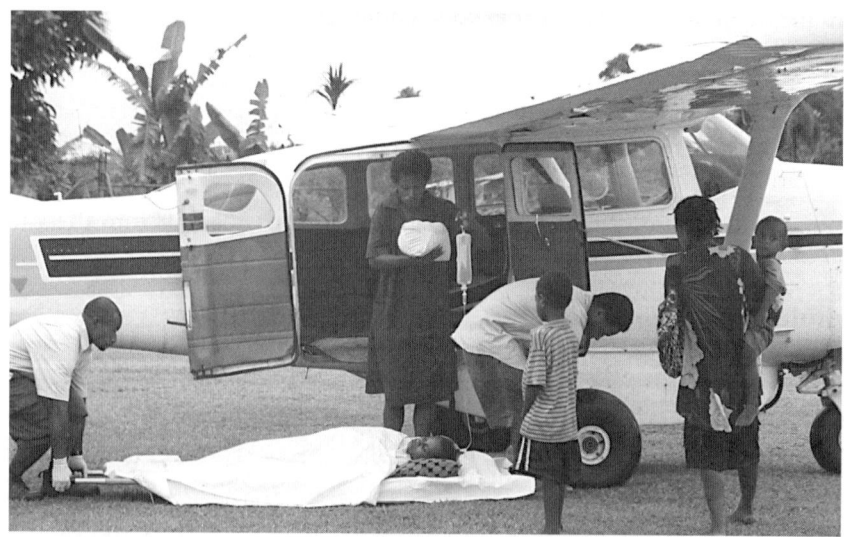

In the same way, you must spend time carefully seeing what the passage DOES say.

Now look at the picture again. What does the picture NOT tell you? For example, you do not know what the sick person is suffering with.

In the same way DO NOT guess about what the passage does NOT say.

Go through verse by verse. Read each verse and then say what happens in your own words. This helps you to know what the passage is about.

Here are some questions to ask:

WHO? *Who is in this passage?*
- What do you learn about each of the people?
- What do you learn about where they are?
- What does this passage say about God?

WHAT? *What is it about?*
- Are any words or ideas repeated?
- Are there things you do not understand?
- If so, pray and read the verses again. Read the whole chapter and see if it becomes clear. There may be some notes in this book or in your Bible that will help you.

WHY? *Why is it said?*
- What does the writer want the hearer to do? For example, in Deuteronomy, what does Moses want the people of Israel to do?
- What difference will it make to God's people? At the end of Deuteronomy we see that the people of Israel obeyed God's commands. They trusted God and followed Joshua into the promised land.

5. Find the MAIN POINT

Find the Main point. The **MAIN POINT** is the big thing God says in each passage. It is important that you find this **IN** the passage.

Some preachers decide what the big thing they want to say is before they start studying the verses! I heard a sermon where the preacher said a lot about giving money. The passage he preached from did not mention giving or money at all! He missed the **MAIN POINT**!

Look at the picture of the plane again:

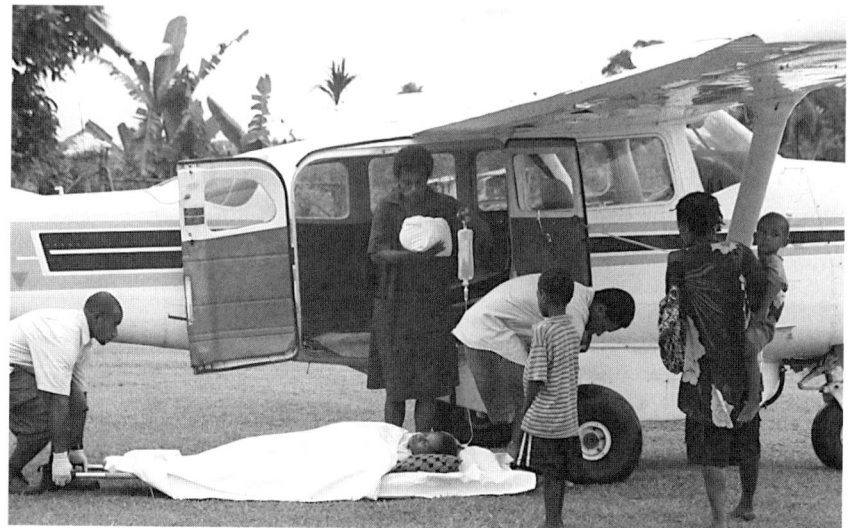

There are many things that you could say about this picture. For example:

- The plane is small.
- The plane has three wheels and some windows.
- There are seven people.

However, none of these things tell us the BIG THING that the picture shows. The big thing is a sick person is being rescued and taken to receive more care.

Sometimes our sermons and talks are like that. They say many true things, but they miss the **MAIN POINT**. Sometimes we want to say everything in a passage. We say so many things that nobody knows what the most important thing is!

The important question to ask is: What is the MAIN POINT, the BIG THING these verses say?

For example, if you preached from Deuteronomy 1:19-33, you could talk about sending someone to look at the land before you go on a long journey. But that is not the **MAIN POINT** of the passage. The passage is about trusting God's promises even when we have strong enemies.

To help you find the main point, read through all you have written in **Notes** and **Something to work on**. Think about the big thing that it says. Look for words or themes that are repeated.

In the picture, the focus was on the sick person being taken onto the plane to get help.

What is the focus of the passage?

Write in one sentence what the passage is about.

For example, if you are preaching from Deuteronomy 1:19-33, you might write: *When you are afraid of strong enemies and find it hard to trust God, remember that God is stronger!*

Write out your **MAIN POINT** and then read the passage again. Make sure you did not leave out anything important.

PLAN

Before you prepare your talk, you will need to PLAN what you will say. We think there are five things you must do:

Main point   Sub-points   Illustrate   Apply   Review

Now you understand the passage. You have some notes and the MAIN POINT—but this is not a sermon or a talk! We need to plan the sermon or talk.

Write the MAIN POINT at the top of your paper. This will help you to plan a good message.

Many preachers do not plan their messages.

Some repeat the same point again and again, which becomes boring. The talk goes round and round in circles! It is unhelpful. Like being on a plane that goes round in circles, but never lands!

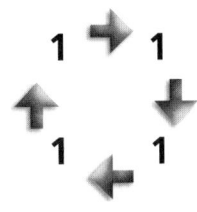

Others have a lot to say but there is no plan. It is hard to follow. Like being on a bus that goes to lots of places but never reaches where you want to go!

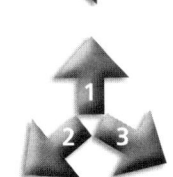

A good way to plan your message is to have two, three or four sub-points or headings. It makes it easy to follow. It is like following the recipe for your favourite soup. You add one thing, then another, then another, until you have a good meal that fills your stomach and satisfies you!

1. Sub-points

Sub-points explain a part of the MAIN POINT.
Sub-points explain one part of the passage.
Sub-points are short so your hearers can remember them.

Think how you will break the passage up.

- What verses go with each of the sub-points?
- Are all the verses covered?
- How can you make the sub-points follow on from each other to make the main point as clear as possible?
- Are the sub-points short and easy to remember?

For example, Deuteronomy 4:9-20:

The main point is: *God has no physical form. So do not worship idols.*

From this, the sub-points might be:

1. Remember what happened at Horeb (Mount Sinai) (4:9-14).
2. Do not make idols (v15-20).
3. Listen to God's words (v9).

Notice that all of the sub-points:

- are short.
- are easy to remember.
- give the meaning of some of these verses.

2. Illustrate or tell a story

An illustration or a word picture helps your hearers understand the main points you make.

Sometimes there are illustrations in the passage.

Sometimes you need to think of your own illustration. Make sure the illustration is easy to understand. For example, if you teach Deuteronomy 16:1-17, the main point is: *God's people must remember what God has done for them, and celebrate.*

The main message is to "remember". Your main illustration or story will show your hearers how important it is to remember!

Tell your hearers how *you* remember and celebrate what has happened—for example, when your church began or when independence came to your country.

You could take a visual aid or picture. You could draw a picture or do a short drama. Always make sure it helps to teach the MAIN POINT!

3. Apply

When we teach God's word, we want God's word to speak to us and change all who hear it. So you must think how the MAIN POINT of the passage applies to the people YOU will speak to.

Think of the different people that you will speak to. How does the MAIN POINT speak to:

- children?
- new believers?
- those who are not believers?
- church leaders?

Think about the questions your listeners will have as they listen. For example:

- What will this mean for me tomorrow?
- How do I put this into practice in this church?
- How will I obey this in my family?
- How will I live this in my village or community?
- How does this help me to follow Jesus faithfully?
- What dangers do I need to be aware of?

You can apply the message after each sub-point and at the end. If you only apply the message at the end, some may not hear it.

You are now ready to write out your sermon or talk.

4. Review

Before you teach it you must review what you wrote.

Check what you prepared:

- Is the main point clear?
- Do you show what the Bible teaches in THAT passage?
- Have you explained the verses clearly?
- Have you thought of word pictures to help people understand and remember the message?
- Do you have a clear flow to your talk so that people can follow what you say?
- What are you asking God to change in the lives of your hearers?

Decide if you will speak using a sermon you wrote out fully or use shorter notes.

Always use the language most of your hearers will understand best.

TEACH

Mostly you will see the following headings in the TEACH section:

Start   2 or 3 Sub-points   Pray

Sometimes there is **Illustrate** or **Apply** in this part as well.

This section will help you write a sermon or talk on the Bible passage. It is not a complete sermon. You will need to do your own work as well—but it gives you ideas. You must take the ideas and use them in the best way for you.

Always remember that the talk is based on the **MAIN POINT**.

1. Start

Think carefully about how to start your talk. It is good to tell your people the main point. Tell them why they need to listen, and how this passage will help them. You can ask a question and tell them that you will answer it in your talk. You need to get their interest so that they will listen.

For example, for Deuteronomy 8:1-20, the main point is: *Remember that God humbled you in the desert. Be humble in the promised land.*

To start, you may ask the question:

- *Do bad times or good times lead people away from God?*

You might tell them a story:

- *A man's wife dies and he has no job. He is angry and complains to God. He loses his faith. A woman finds her life is good. She gets more things and is rich. But then she moves away from God.*

2. Sub-points

Sub-points are like bones in a body. They keep you standing up straight. But you also need flesh or meat! You need to take time to explain the verses, to put meat on the bones. You need to make clear what the verses mean. It is good to keep reading out the verses from the Bible as you explain them. Get your people to follow in their Bibles if they have them.

This book gives you some ideas, but you will also need to add your own. Think of what is good for your people and what will help them to understand clearly.

Make sure your hearers can see that what you say is what the Bible says!

3. Illustrate

In the TEACH section there may be an illustration. You may need to think of others also. This is what Jesus did when he told parables. Jesus often said, "The kingdom of heaven is *like...*" and then told a story. Some of the illustrations Jesus used were word pictures. For example, he speaks of false teachers as "dangerous wolves". Paul spoke of the Christian life as "running a race". Sometimes a word picture is better than a long story.

4. Apply

You will need to apply the passage to your hearers. It is important to make this as clear as possible. Give your hearers something to think about, or something to do. Remember, we want people to change and grow. Make sure you remember to say something to those who are not believers. You always have different groups of people listening:

- Believers who are full of faith
- Believers who are struggling to keep going
- Unbelievers who want to become Christians but do not know how
- Unbelievers who do not think they need to be saved

Try to say something to each one! Everyone needs to hear something.

For example, when teaching Deuteronomy 4:21-31:

- To believers who are full of faith: *You belong to God. God is jealous for you, and does not want you to love money instead of him.*

- To believers who are struggling to keep going: *God is merciful and will forgive you, even if you have failed. He loves you.*
- To unbelievers who want to become Christians but do not know how: *God is full of mercy. He forgives failures—even bad failures. You will be forgiven if you turn from your sin and turn back to God.*
- To unbelievers who do not think they need to be saved: *God is a jealous God. He hates people who serve idols, and will judge them.*

Make sure how you apply is based on how the passage applied to the person, or people, who first read it. For example, with Deuteronomy 5:12-15:

- Some people are lazy. The law says that they must work 6 days. *What should we be working hard at every day?*
- Some people work too hard because they are greedy. *God tells us that we must rest and enjoy the world and the life we have been given.*

5. End

Think how to end your talk. Remind your hearers of the main point. Help them to remember.

Sometimes it is helpful after speaking to give your hearers time to think and pray about what they heard, before you carry on with the meeting.

6. Pray

Pray, and keep praying!

- Pray that God will first change you.
- Pray that God will use your words to speak to your people.
- Pray that God's truth will change your people.

C. About the book of Deuteronomy

LAST SERMON

Deuteronomy is Moses' last sermon before he died. Moses preaches to all the people of Israel, on a mountain outside the promised land of Canaan.

The people of Israel have been almost 40 years in the desert after they left Egypt. (See Exodus 14:37-41.) Because the people of Israel decide not to enter the promised land, God says all the adults will die in the desert. Later, their children will enter the land. (See Numbers 13 – 14.)

All the time in the desert, the people of Israel disobeyed God and went against him. (See Exodus 15:22-26, 16:1-3, 17:1-7; Numbers 11:1-3, 14:1-4, 20:2-5, 25:1-3.)

WHAT DOES MOSES WANT TO DO?

Moses is about to die. Joshua will become the leader of the Israelites. Joshua will lead the Israelites into the land. So Moses preaches a long sermon. He wants to do four things:

1. To remind them of their past.
2. To increase their faith in God.
3. To help them obey his laws.
4. To encourage them to conquer the land.

Deuteronomy is this sermon.

The land is called the promised land because 600 years earlier, God promised this land to Abraham. (See Genesis 12:1-7.) The book of Deuteronomy makes it clear that God is faithful to those promises.

WHY MUST PEOPLE OBEY GOD'S LAWS?

Much of Deuteronomy is about laws to obey, but the book always brings our attention to God. The people of Israel must obey God's law from their hearts for three reasons.

1. Because of what God did for the people of Israel in the past.
2. Because of who God is.
3. Because of the promises of God and because of his warnings for the future.

WHAT DOES DEUTERONOMY SAY TO US?

The book of Deuteronomy speaks to the people of Israel. Moses wrote down his sermon in a book so that future generations can read it and find God speaks to them also.

This same book speaks to us as Christians, those who follow Christ. We are not a nation like Israel but a church. Christians are the descendants of Abraham by faith. So the main way this book applies today is to God's people, the Christian church.

That means we need to think carefully how to apply laws to our different situations. We must read them in the light of Jesus and the New Testament. (For help, see the appendix on reading Old Testament laws, page 98.)

Moses aimed to encourage the people of Israel to faithful obedience. This sermon has the same aim for us. It is to encourage us to be faithful and obey God.

Outline of the book

1:1-5	Introduction
1:6 – 4:43	Historical background
4:44 – 11:32	General commands
12:1 – 26:19	Detailed laws
27:1 – 28:68	Blessings and curses
29:1 – 30:20	Conclusion
31:1 – 34:12	Moses prepares to hand over to Joshua and die

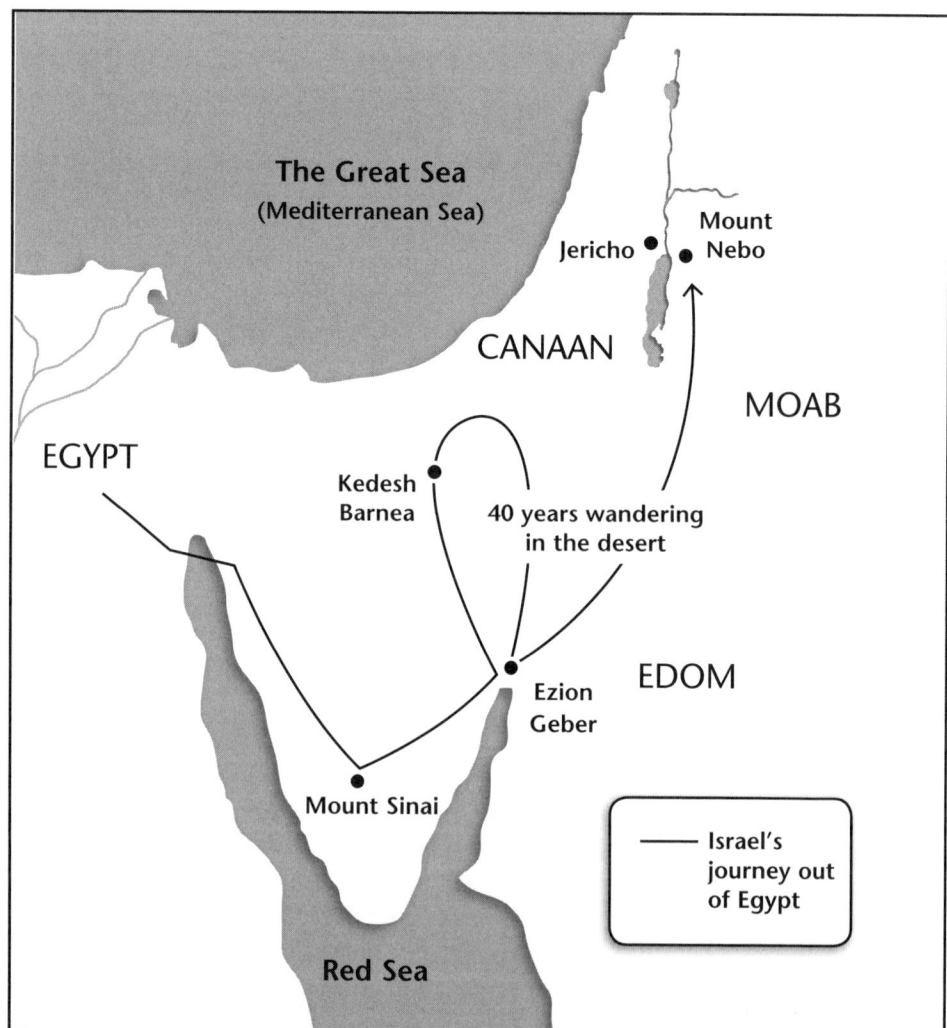

TEACHING DEUTERONOMY

D: Study and teach the book of Deuteronomy

STUDY: Deuteronomy 1:1-8

1 ENTER THE LAND

Background
These verses give the background to the book of Deuteronomy. They say:
- **Who the book is from:** Moses led the Israelites out of Egypt and through the desert for 40 years.
- **Who the book is to:** All the people of Israel, every person, young and old, male and female.
- **What the book is:** Words spoken by Moses (v1), commanded by God (v3).
- **Where the sermon was spoken:** On the other side of the Jordan river, outside the promised land.
- **When the words were spoken:** In the 40th year after leaving Egypt.
- **Why Deuteronomy is needed:** To explain God's law (v5).

Read verses 1-8.
Read the passage 2 or 3 times. Read each verse and explain it to yourself in your own words. This helps you know what the passage is about.

Notes
- **Deuteronomy 1:4.** The defeat of Sihon and Og is in Numbers 21:21-26.
- **Deuteronomy 1:5.** "Law." The word for law in Hebrew means "instruction" or "way of living".
- **Deuteronomy 1:7.** The Arabah (NIV) is the lower Jordan valley. The western foothills (Shephelah) are in the middle of the country. See the map on page 18.

Something to work on
Read the promises that God made about the land: to Abraham in Genesis 12:1-7, 15:13-18; to Isaac in Genesis 26:2-5; to Jacob in Genesis 28:12-15. See how this promise was passed on, and still applies to the people of Israel in Deuteronomy.

Think how faith and obedience belong together. The Israelites are to trust God's promise to give them the land. That means they must obey the command to take the land from their enemies. So when we preach to help God's people obey, we must increase their faith in God. If we do not make faith important, then we make Christianity into a religion of laws.

For true Christians, our "promised land" is heavenly (eg: 1 Peter 1:4).

- *How do faith and obedience work together for us? (For example, James 2:14-26.)*

⊕ MAIN POINT
God commands his people to enter the land he has promised.

◉ TEACH: Deuteronomy 1:1-8

◈ Start
- How do you encourage Christians to obey God more?

Moses encourages the people of Israel by keeping the focus on God—and especially God's promises. The people of Israel often failed. Christian encouragement needs to follow God and not people.

Introduction of the book
◉ Read: *Deuteronomy 1:1-5*
Tell your listeners the background to the book. Explain the key things: Who, to whom, what, where and when from verses 1-5. Then focus on why.

Why did Moses preach this sermon? To encourage the people of Israel to trust God's promises and obey God's law.

The main task
◉ Read: *Deuteronomy 1:6-8*
God commands the people of Israel to enter the promised land. Verse 7 tells us what is included in the land. Verse 8 tells us that the land was promised to Abraham, Isaac and Jacob. That promise was made 600 years before Moses. Yet the promise still stands in Moses' day.

The Israelites will only obey God and enter the land if they trust God's promise to give them the land.

ⓘ Apply:
God promised the Israelites a land on earth. This was a model of the heavenly land that is promised by God for true Christians. Earthly land is not important in the same way for Christians. Christians are on the way to a heavenly land. Do we trust God's promise that he will give believers a heavenly land? How does this promise help you and me to obey God's commands now?

✦ Illustration:
Imagine you promise your child a very special present next year. But your child keeps asking for sweets now. You say to your child that he or she must wait for the much greater present next year. You remind them how good the present will be. Let us not be like children, wanting small things now. Let us be good and patient, waiting for the much greater treasure of heaven.

So, when we are tempted to want more money, we must think of the much greater treasure that is in heaven. When we are tempted to live for fun, we must think about the greater joy there will be in heaven.

⬆ Pray:
Ask God to help you keep your mind on the promise of heaven, so that you will have strength to obey him on earth.

⬇ STUDY: Deuteronomy 1:9-18

2 SO MANY ISRAELITES

ⓘ Background
Moses reminds the people of God's command to enter the promised land. God first made the promise of land to Abraham in Genesis 12:1-7. At that time, it was only Abraham and his wife. Now there are many Israelites descended from Abraham.

So many Israelites means that God is faithful. So many Israelites means Moses needs helpers to judge the people.

⊙ Read verses 9-18.
Read the passage 2 or 3 times.

ⓘ Notes
- **Deuteronomy 1:10-11.** "Stars in the sky" refers to the promise given to Abraham in Genesis 15:5. Notice in verse 11 the reminder of "as he (God) has promised".
- **Deuteronomy 1:12-18.** Read Exodus 18:13-27 for the background to this. Because God has kept his promise of many people, there is too much work for Moses to do by himself.
- **Deuteronomy 1:13, 16-17.** God's leaders are to treat everybody in the same way. "Partiality" means to treat people in different ways, to show favour to some more than others.
- **Deuteronomy 1:16.** "Alien" (GN: "foreigner"). This means a person from another country but who wants to be a permanent resident in Israel.

⊙ Something to work on
Read Genesis 15:1-6, 18-21.
- *What two promises are here?*

Deuteronomy 1:10 says Israel is now as numerous as the stars of the sky.
- *Where does that quote come from?*

In Genesis 15, Abraham doubted God's promises, so God assured him. Moses does not want the people of Israel to doubt the promises. God kept the promise of many descendants to Abraham, which means the people can trust God to keep the promise of land also.

Because there are many Israelites, Moses needs helpers to judge the people.
- *What sort of people will they be (v13, 16-17)?*

Read Deuteronomy 10:17-18. Leaders are to have the same attitude as God. Leaders must not be afraid of the people but do what is right in God's eyes.

⊕ MAIN POINT
Trust God. He keeps his promises.

➡ TEACH: Deuteronomy 1:9-18

⊙ Start
When people make promises and keep them, then when they make another promise, you are likely to trust them.

- When has that happened for you?

Promises fulfilled in part
⊙ Read: Deuteronomy 1:10
In Genesis 12 God promised Abraham many descendants and land. Later, Abraham doubted those promises so God reminded him in Genesis 15. God promised that Abraham's descendants will be as many as the stars in the sky. Abraham changed from doubt to faith.

The people of Israel doubted the promise of land. Because of that they failed to enter the land. Now Moses reminds the people of Israel, as God reminded Abraham. Already the people of Israel are as many as the stars in the sky. So they can be very sure that God will also carry out the promise to give them the land.

- Do you feel you can trust God? How has God shown his faithfulness to his promises to you?

Moses appoints leaders
⊙ Read: Deuteronomy 1:12-18
The number of Israelites was so many that Moses needed to choose leaders to help him. The leaders must be wise and be respected by God's people. They must treat everyone the same way.

So we need to make sure that church leaders are fair and just.

⊕ Illustration: Sadly, in many places the church shows unjust and unfair treatment. In some countries, the appointment of a church leader is made only because of the bribes paid to the people who vote. This is not what God wants.

⊙ Apply: How do we make sure we treat everyone the same? This is very hard when relatives and rich people expect to be first, and get angry when they do not get their own way. Do people who give money to the church become the leaders? How can we choose leaders so that our leaders are wise, understanding, fair and just?

Verse 17 says do not be afraid of people. Sometimes we are too afraid of what other people will think or do. We must make decisions that are right in God's eyes.

⊙ Pray: *Ask God to help us trust his promises. Ask God to help us always to be just and fair in our leadership and to choose the right leaders.*

ⓓ STUDY: Deuteronomy 1:19-33

3 LEARN FROM PARENTS

ⓜ Background
Moses is preaching to the people of Israel. They are on the edge of the promised land. Moses wants to encourage them to take the land from their enemies. He reminds the people that their parents did not enter the land. They disobeyed God. (Numbers 13 – 14.) Their mothers and fathers died in the desert. Moses preaches so that the Israelites do not make the same mistake.

ⓡ Read verses 19-33.
Read each verse and explain it to yourself in your own words.

ⓝ Notes
• **Deuteronomy 1:19.** Kadesh Barnea was the border town to the south of the promised land. This is where the parents disobeyed and did not enter the land. See the map on page 18.
• **Deuteronomy 1:21, 25, 30.** Notice the land is promised, "given", and God fights for Israel. "Hesitate" (v21, GN) means hold back.
• **Deuteronomy 1:25.** What the spies said was positive. They agreed that the land was good. "Fertile" (GN) means that fruit and trees grow well there. They agreed God was giving the land to the Israelites.
• **Deuteronomy 1:28.** The parents feared two things about the enemies in the land: they were strong and they had cities protected by strong walls. The Anakites (NIV) were very tall people (giants) who made the people of Israel afraid.

⊙ Something to work on
Think about the disobedience of their parents—their fathers and mothers. Their sin is seen in 1:27-28. Their sin is explained in two ways.

1. They rebelled against God and disobeyed him (v26).

2. They did not trust in God (v32). Their sin is having no faith.
• *How do disobeying God and not trusting him go together?*

The people are afraid of the enemy.
• *How does Moses try to help the people get rid of their fear?*

See what Moses says in verses 29-31. The same idea is also in verse 21.

• *Think of the situations your church members have that need the same encouragement.*

⊕ MAIN POINT
We must trust God's promises even when we have strong enemies. God is much stronger.

→ TEACH: Deuteronomy 1:19-33

> Start

The Israelites' parents disobeyed when they arrived at the promised land. Moses does not want the people now to make the same mistake. How will the Israelites be encouraged to enter and take the land? They must not think they are better than their parents! They need to trust God.

The sin of the parents
⊙ Read: *Deuteronomy 1:27-28*

Their parents disobeyed because they were afraid of the enemy. They did not trust God. Their parents said:

- "God hates us" (v27).
- "The enemy is too strong" (v28).
- "The enemy is well protected" (v28).

The first point is not true. When we forget what God has promised us and done for us, we can think God hates us. We forget that God loves us.

The second and third points are true! The enemy is powerful. But the people of Israel forgot that God is much more powerful.

The parents of the Israelites sinned. This sin is explained in two ways:

1. They rebelled against God (v26).
2. They had no trust in God (v32).

- What enemies make you afraid?

Maybe governments, non-believing family members, a boss at work or a witchdoctor? Do you forget God's power and faithfulness?

Do not let this happen again
⊙ Read: *Deuteronomy 1:30-31*

Do not think you are better than your parents! Moses encourages the Israelites to think about God:

- Now God goes before you (v30).
- God will fight for you (v30).
- God did this before (v30-31).

The enemy is strong but God is stronger. God will defeat any enemy to keep his promise. We can have victory against enemies of God's promises. God promises believing Christians a heavenly land. On the cross, Jesus defeated all enemies. Jesus made sure all true Christians will arrive in heaven.

- Are you afraid that Satan or magicians or enemies can stop you going to heaven?

Your enemy is strong but God is much stronger! Jesus has already won. All of God's people will enter the promised land of heaven.

⊕ **Illustration:** Imagine the local authority says your church must stop meeting. You are afraid of the authorities. So you stop the church from meeting. Do not be afraid of enemies. God is much stronger!

⊕ **Pray:** *Ask God to help you not be afraid of enemies.*

⬇ STUDY: Deuteronomy 1:34-46

4 GOD'S JUDGMENT

⊛ Background
Moses is reminding the people of Israel of the time when their parents disobeyed God. In verses 26-33, Moses explained the sin of the parents. Moses now speaks of God's judgment.

⊙ Read verses 34-45.
Read each verse and explain it to yourself in your own words.

⊛ Notes
- **Deuteronomy 1:34.** "Solemnly declared/swore" means strongly said.
- **Deuteronomy 1:39.** "Seized" (GN) means taken away. The children did not know what was right or wrong. They were not punished for their parents' sin. They will enter the land only because God will keep his promise.
- **Deuteronomy 1:40.** "Set out towards the desert." The people of Israel went away from the promised land for nearly 40 years.
- **Deuteronomy 1:41.** The people said they had sinned but kept on disobeying God! "Thinking it easy to go up" (NIV). The people of Israel thought they could defeat the enemy without God's help.

⊙ Something to work on
Some people think God can never be angry. But God is angry at sin (v34). Because God is holy, he hates sin and is unhappy when people sin. God's anger is always right. Our anger is often sinful, when we are angry for selfish or proud reasons.

Who will enter the promised land? God punished the parents for their sin. They all died in the desert. Caleb and Joshua will enter the promised land because they were faithful (Numbers 14:6-10). Even Moses will not enter the land because he sinned (Numbers 20:2-12). The children will enter the land (Deuteronomy 1:39). God will keep his promise even though the parents sinned. Verse 35 mentions God's promise to the "forefathers" ("ancestors", GN); that is, Abraham.

Moses tells how the parents heard God's judgment but they decided to enter the land anyway (v41-46). But it was too late. God told them not to go (v42). God did not go with them. They lost to their enemies and were chased away from the land.

⊕ MAIN POINT
God judges sin but he still keeps his promises.

◉ TEACH: Deuteronomy 1:34-46

⊕ Illustration
Imagine two men. One gets angry when he does not get what he wants. Another man is angry because his government ignores poor people. Is there a difference in their anger? The first man's anger is selfish and wrong. The second man's anger is just and good.

God gets angry. God is angry when people sin. His anger is like the second man's anger.

Punishment for sin
⊙ Read: *Deuteronomy 1:35, 37*
The parents of the Israelites did not trust and obey God (Deuteronomy 1:26, 32). God's punishment was they cannot enter the land. Even Moses cannot enter because he also sinned when he struck the rock in the desert to get water (Numbers 20:2-12).

God still keeps his promise
⊙ Read: *Deuteronomy 1:36, 38-39*
Explain why Caleb and Joshua will enter the land.

Why will the children enter the land? Not because they are better than their parents. They will enter because God keeps his promise to Abraham (v35).

Christians are heading for a heavenly land. We will not be there because we are good. We will be there because God keeps his promises. He promises that all those who repent and trust in Jesus will be in heaven. So we must repent of our sin. We must love and live for Jesus. We must please him by trying not to sin.

The people sin again
⊙ Read: *Deuteronomy 1:41-45*
The parents later decided to enter the land but God was not with them. They should have obeyed the first time. With God, they were sure of victory. Without God, they were sure of defeat.

Our enemy is Satan, who aims to stop us arriving in heaven. We cannot defeat Satan on our own. We need God. Jesus has already defeated Satan. So we should trust Jesus' victory.

⊕ **Illustration:** God called a man to follow him. But the man said no. He did not want to follow God. He thought he would turn to God at the end of his life. But it was too late. God ended his life before he had another chance.

⊙ **Apply:** Do not delay obeying God. And do not think you can arrive in heaven by your own strength. You need to trust in Jesus' victory.

⬇ STUDY: Deuteronomy 2:1 – 3:11

5 GOD ENCOURAGES HIS PEOPLE

✎ Background
Moses is encouraging the people of Israel to enter and take the promised land. He reminds them of five nations the people of Israel met. The Israelites passed by three nations without fighting. These were Edom, Moab and Ammon. Then they won battles against two other nations, Heshbon and Bashan.

⊙ Read 2:1 – 3:11.
Read each verse and explain it to yourself in your own words.

✎ Notes
- **Deuteronomy 2:4.** The people of Edom were descended from Esau, who was the twin brother of Jacob in Genesis.
- **Deuteronomy 2:9, 19.** The people of Moab and Ammon were descended from Lot, who was the nephew of Abraham in Genesis.
- **Deuteronomy 2:10-11, 20-21.** "Anakites / Anakim", "Rephaites / Rephaim": People of old times who were very tall (giants). The people of Israel were afraid of the Anakites (1:28).

⊙ Something to work on
Look at the map on page 18 to see the five nations. You can also read Numbers 20:14-21, 21:10-13, 21-35.

God gave Edom, Moab and Ammon their lands (Deuteronomy 2:5, 9, 19). That was why the people of Israel must not fight them.

God promises to give the people of Israel their land also. There were very tall people in the land of Moab and Ammon before (2:10-11, 20-21). God defeated the tall people to give Moab and Ammon their land.

Remember the parents of the Israelites were afraid of tall people in 1:28. Moses wanted the people of Israel to trust that God is strong enough to defeat giants.

Israel defeated King Sihon of Heshbon and King Og of Bashan. God did not give them their land. Sihon and Og had many strong cities (2:36; 3:4). Remember that the Israelite parents were afraid of strong cities in 1:28. Moses wanted the people of Israel to trust that God is strong enough to defeat strong cities.

King Og was also a giant. That is why his bed was so big (3:11). But he was also killed. God is stronger than giants.

⊕ MAIN POINT
God has worked in the past, so be encouraged.

➔ TEACH: Deuteronomy 2:1 – 3:11

⊙ Start
- What are some things God has done for you before?

Give some examples of what God has done. Maybe he has provided for you in a special way. Maybe he has answered prayers very clearly.

- Does it encourage you for the future?

Moses reminds Israel of what God has done in the past. He encourages them to face the future with faith.

God defeated strong people
⊙ Read: *2:10-11, 20-21*

Tell your listeners about the nations of Edom, Moab and Ammon. Show that God gave these nations their land.

Now show that there were giants in their lands before.

God defeated giants to give the nations their land. God is much stronger than giants.

- **God can still defeat tall and strong people.**

Moses tells the people of Israel about the past so they trust that God is strong to defeat giants in their land when they enter. The parents were afraid of giants (1:28) and did not enter the land.

- **Moses encourages faith because of what God did in the past.**

God defeated strong cities
⊙ Read: *2:36, 3:4*

Tell your listeners about the nations of Sihon and Og. Show that the Israelites defeated them before. It was God's power that won the battle. God defeated strong cities before.

- **God can still defeat strong cities.**

Moses tells the people of Israel about this so they will trust that God is strong to defeat strong cities as they enter their land. Their parents were afraid of the strong cities of their enemies (1:28) and did not enter the land.

- **Moses encourages faith because of what God did in the past.**

God is still the same today! He is strong and can defeat every enemy.

Jesus defeated all our enemies on the cross. Jesus defeated sin, Satan and death. We should have strong faith in God and trust God to help us.

⚠ **Apply:** Remember what Jesus has done in the past. Think of how God has already helped you. He will help you again and again. Trust him always!

⇧ **Pray:** *Ask God to help you remember his strength so you can trust him every day.*

STUDY: Deuteronomy 3:23-29

6 EVEN LEADERS FAIL

⊗ Background
Deuteronomy is the last sermon Moses preaches. Soon he will die. Moses will not enter the promised land because he sinned before. He warns the people of Israel so they do not sin.

⊙ Read verses 23-29.
Read the passage 2 or 3 times. Read each verse and explain it to yourself in your own words.

⊗ Notes
• **Deuteronomy 3:23.** Moses remembers how he strongly ("earnestly", GN) asked God to let him enter the land.

• **Deuteronomy 3:26.** Moses refers to the sin of the people that made him angry. Then Moses sinned and God was angry with him.

• **Deuteronomy 3:27.** "Pisgah." The name of the mountain area where Moses will die (Deuteronomy 34:1).

• **Deuteronomy 3:27.** Moses is able to see the promised land but not enter it. See Deuteronomy 34:1-4.

• **Deuteronomy 3:28.** Joshua was one of the twelve spies (1:22-23). He was faithful (1:38). "Commission" means to pray, and send a leader.

⊙ Something to work on
The sin of Moses is in Numbers 20:2-13. Moses was angry with the people. Moses struck the rock twice. Moses said he, and not God, would bring water from the rock (v10). This was a serious sin. Moses did not trust God and did not show God's holiness to the people of Israel (v12).
• *Who was to blame for Moses' sin?*

Moses could blame the people. The people made him angry. But the fault belonged to Moses. Moses was guilty of sin because he did not trust in God and honour God.

God punishes Moses by not letting him enter the land. Moses will die at the end of Deuteronomy. Joshua will lead the people into the land.
• *Is the punishment of Moses fair?*

Moses did many great things for God. Moses was a servant of God. Should God have let Moses enter the land? Moses wanted to enter the land very much. God's judgment is fair. The sin of Moses was serious. This is a warning to us that God takes all sin seriously.

⊕ MAIN POINT
Even God's leaders fail.

➲ TEACH: Deuteronomy 3:23-29

⊙ Start
Sometimes we think God's leaders are perfect. It is good for Christians to know that even leaders fail. *Tell your listeners of some of the leaders in the Bible who failed: Abraham, Samson, David, Solomon.*

Moses sinned. *Explain to your listeners what the sin of Moses was. Tell them his sin was serious because he did not give God the honour for bringing water from the rock.* Moses was not allowed to enter the promised land.

Moses prayed to enter the promised land
⊙ **Read: *Deuteronomy 3:23-25***
Moses speaks of God's greatness (v24). God has done great and powerful things. Moses remembers how he asked God to let him enter the land (v25). Moses asked God to give him mercy. Mercy means forgiveness. Moses wanted God to ignore his sin.

God answers Moses' prayer
⊙ **Read: *Deuteronomy 3:26-29***
God answered "No" (v26). Moses cannot enter the promised land. God does not always say "Yes" to our prayers. God will not always give us mercy. God is holy. The people made Moses angry. But that is no excuse for his sin.

God gives two more answers to the prayer of Moses.
1. Moses is allowed to see the land (v27). Moses will go up this mountain to die (Deuteronomy 34:1). This shows God's kindness to Moses.

2. Joshua will lead the people after Moses dies (v28). This is also God's kindness for the people of Israel. God will give them another leader.

Warnings for us
The sin of Moses warns us. Even God's leaders fail. We must not think God will always give mercy. We must trust and obey God always. If other people make us angry, that is no excuse for us to sin. We must still obey and trust God.

⊕ **Illustration:** A man's wife was late cooking dinner. It made her husband angry. So the husband beat his wife. Their pastor heard about it and spoke to the husband. The husband said it was his wife's fault because the dinner was late. The pastor told the man he was wrong. If someone makes us angry, we do not have an excuse to sin.

⊕ **Pray:** *Ask God to help the leaders of God's people trust and obey God always.*

STUDY: Deuteronomy 4:1-8

7 OBEY SO OTHERS WILL BELIEVE

Background
Moses is reminding the people of Israel about the past. This is because he wants them to obey God and enter the promised land. Now Moses begins to tell them how to live. He gives them one warning and one encouragement.

Read verses 1-8.
Read the passage 2 or 3 times. Read each verse and explain it to yourself in your own words.

Notes
- **Deuteronomy 4:2.** "Do not add ... and do not subtract" (NIV) or "take anything away" (GN). We must never change God's word. Sometimes God's word is hard to obey, but we must not change it to make it easy.

- **Deuteronomy 4:7.** "The LORD our God is near us" (NIV). When the Israelites obey, then God will bless them. God will be close to them. Other nations will see this and be amazed.

- **Deuteronomy 4:8.** "Righteous decrees and laws" (NIV). The law of God given in the Old Testament is very fair. The law of God is much better than the laws of other nations. Other nations will come to God when Israel obeys God's law.

Something to work on
Read what happened to the people of Israel at Peor in Numbers 25:1-9. The people of Israel did sexual sin and idolatry.

The warning for the people of Israel is they must not follow the bad ways of others. The encouragement for the people of Israel is when they obey God, others might follow them and come to God.

God chose Abraham, the ancestor of the people of Israel, so that the nations of the world would be blessed through him (Genesis 12:3).

Deuteronomy 4:6-8 explains how that will happen. When the people of Israel obey God, other people or nations will ask questions and be amazed about Israel and God.

The people of Israel were a nation. Today God's people are the church. God's people live in all the nations. Think how the church must obey God and attract people to God.

MAIN POINT
When God's people obey God, other people will come to God.

⊙ TEACH: Deuteronomy 4:1-8

⊙ Start
- Do you think the way Christians live is different from how others live?

Sadly there is often no difference. The people of God sometimes lie, are unjust, greedy and do other wrong things. God's people must be different from non-believers. This is so non-believers will come to God.

✣ Illustration: When an unbelieving neighbour of a Christian was sick, the Christian bought food, cooked meals and helped the sick neighbour. The unbeliever was amazed. When she heard that her neighbour was so kind because she was a Christian, the sick lady also wanted to be a Christian.

Warning!
Do not follow others
⊙ **Read: *Deuteronomy 4:3-4***
Tell your listeners about the sin at Peor from Numbers 25:1-9. Explain that the people of Israel followed the idolatry and sexual sins of the unbelievers at Peor. Remind your listeners that God punished the Israelites by death.

Christians must not follow the sins of our world. God's people must live by God's standards. For example, we must not worship idols, spirits and other gods. We must not make money our god. We must always tell the truth. God is not happy when Christians live like unbelievers.

Encouragement!
Obey God and be different
⊙ **Read: *Deuteronomy 4:6-8***
In the promised land, the Israelites must obey God (v1, 5). They must be very different from other nations. What will happen then?

- People of other nations will think the people of Israel are wise (v6).
- People of other nations will see God is close to the people of Israel (v7).
- People of other nations will see Israel's law is just and fair (v8).

God wants to bring the nations to worship him. God will do this through his people. This was why God chose Abraham's family (Israel) in Genesis 12:3.

Today the people of God are Christians. Christians must obey God. Christians must be different from the world. But like the Israelites, Christians often follow the behaviour of unbelievers.

⊙ **Apply:** *Encourage your people to be different from the world and to live in a way that attracts people to God.*

⊙ **Pray:** *Ask God to help your church members obey him and live differently from the world. Ask God to bring people to follow him through the example of Christians.*

⬇ STUDY: Deuteronomy 4:9-20

8 DO NOT WORSHIP IDOLS

❈ Background
Moses is preaching to the people of Israel before they enter the promised land. Moses reminds the people of Israel of the time when they were at Mount Sinai (Horeb).

⊙ Read verses 9-20.
Read each verse and explain it to yourself in your own words.

❈ Notes
- **Deuteronomy 4:10.** "Horeb" (NIV) is another name for Sinai.
- **Deuteronomy 4:12.** God spoke to the people "out of/from the fire". The people did not see God, but they heard his voice. The fire showed that God was present.
- **Deuteronomy 4:15.** "Watch yourselves very carefully" (NIV). This means it will not be easy for the people of Israel to obey this command.
- **Deuteronomy 4:16.** "Corrupt" (NIV) means to do wrong.
- **Deuteronomy 4:20.** "Iron-smelting/blazing furnace" refers to making idols from metal in Egypt. "Inheritance" refers to the special relationship God has at that time with the people of Israel.

⊙ Something to work on
The people of Israel came to Mount Sinai (Exodus 19). They stayed there for about one year. God spoke to them and gave them the laws.

Most religions then had idols for worship. They were made of wood or stone. Idols often looked like people, animals, snakes, birds or fish. Many religions also worshipped the sun, moon and stars. The Israelites were not allowed to have idols.
- *What is the reason for this?*

Verses 16-19 remind us of Genesis 1:14-27. All these things are made by God. We must worship God the creator and not the things he made.

Another reason to worship God is in verse 20. God brought Israel out of Egypt to be his own people. Israel is to be different from other nations.

What God says is more important than what God looks like. We must listen to him. What God has done for his people is more important than what he looks like. He has rescued the Israelites from Egypt.

⊕ MAIN POINT
God has no physical form. So do not worship idols.

⊙ TEACH: Deuteronomy 4:9-20

⊙ Start

Children sometimes ask: "What does God look like?" Is he white or black or Asian? Does he have a beard? We do not know. When the people of Israel were at Horeb, they did not see God. They only heard his voice.

Remember Horeb (Sinai)
⊙ Read: *Deuteronomy 4:9-14*

Moses reminds the people of Israel of when they were at Mount Horeb (Sinai). The people were close to the mountain. There was fire, cloud and darkness. There was the voice of God. But the people did not see God.

God spoke the words of the Ten Commandments and other laws (v14).

The main point of this section is to "remember". God has no physical form. They must not forget. They must tell their children and grandchildren (v9-11).

Do not make idols
⊙ Read: *Deuteronomy 4:15-20*

The people must remember Horeb so that they do not make an idol to worship as God. Many unbelievers have idols.

- In your country, are there religions with idols, statues and pictures for their worship? What do their idols look like?

People make idols from the things listed in verses 16-20. *Show your listeners how these things are mentioned in Genesis 1*. It is bad to worship things that God has made. We are to worship God alone.

The people of Egypt made idols. God brought the people of Israel out from there. For us, God also has rescued believers in Jesus. We must worship God alone.

- Think carefully about your life. Are there other things you worship? Are there other things that take the place of God in your life?

Listen to God's words

Today we hear God's voice by reading God's words in the Bible. God speaks to us in the Bible and we must obey his words. The Bible is God's word for us. So we must pay careful attention to the Bible.

⊕ **Illustration:** Some Christians look at statues or pictures of Jesus or Mary or other people and do not listen to God speaking in the Bible. This is dangerous. It makes people ignorant and superstitious. Christians must pay attention to the words of God in the Bible and obey them carefully.

⊙ **Pray:** *Ask God to help you listen to him when you read the Bible.*

STUDY: Deuteronomy 4:21-31

9 A JEALOUS AND MERCIFUL GOD

Background
Moses is preaching to the people before they enter the promised land. He warned them not to worship idols.

Read verses 21-31.
Read each verse and explain it to yourself in your own words.

Notes
- **Deuteronomy 4:23.** "Covenant" means a firm relationship.

- **Deuteronomy 4:24.** "Jealous" (NIV). Jealous can mean we wrongly want something that belongs to someone else. But here jealous means that God wants what belongs only to him. God's people belong only to him because he rescued them.

- **Deuteronomy 4:26.** "Perish" (NIV) means to be destroyed or die.

- **Deuteronomy 4:29.** "Seek the LORD" (NIV) means turn away from sin and turn back to God for forgiveness. The people must seek God with all their heart and soul. They must really want God.

- **Deuteronomy 4:31.** "Merciful" means that God will forgive and bring the people back to the promised land. They do not deserve this.

Something to work on
- *What are the commands from God in this passage?*

God is jealous (v24). He is angry when his people turn away from him. That is why God was angry with Moses. (See Numbers 20:12 and Deuteronomy 3:26.) So God's people must be careful not to forget the covenant promises.

- *What will God do if the people of Israel turn away from him and worship idols (v26-28)?*

God is also merciful (v31). He wants to forgive his people. The people of Israel must seek the LORD (v29). Then they will come back to the land. Even when God's people turn away from him, God does not forget them because he keeps his promises to Abraham.

Hundreds of years later, God punished Israel because they turned away from him. The people of Babylon defeated Israel. Many Israelites were taken to Babylon. But later, some came back to the land.

MAIN POINT
God is both jealous and merciful.

➔ TEACH: Deuteronomy 4:21-31

⊙ Start
- What is God like? Is he full of love? Is he angry? Can he be both?

God is jealous
⊙ **Read: *Deuteronomy 4:21-28***

✳ **Illustration:** It is right to be jealous for whatever is ours alone. So a husband and wife must be jealous for their partner. They belong only to each other. When a husband finds out his wife loves another man, he is right to be angry. When a wife finds out her husband loves another woman, she is right to be angry.

God is jealous for his people. They belong to him alone. God alone rescued them. When his people turn to other gods and idols, God is angry.

Explain to your listeners that the main command is verse 23: "**Do not forget the covenant**". If the people of Israel make an idol, they forget the covenant. They forget they belong to God alone.

Explain what will happen if God's people forget God (v26-28). Tell your listeners that this is what happened to the people of Israel later.

God is merciful
⊙ **Read: *Deuteronomy 4:29-31***

God is also merciful. God wants his people to seek him. *Explain to your listeners that the people must be sincere, real, from the heart and not just people who pretend or try to trick God.*

If the people turn to God and turn away from their sin, God will bring them back to the land. God will keep his promises to Abraham. God is faithful even when his people are not faithful.

In the New Testament God is jealous and merciful. On the cross, Jesus died for sins because God is angry when people turn away from him. Jesus' death also shows God is merciful and forgives.

⊙ **Apply:** We must keep the covenant with God, and thank God that he forgives our failures. We must be sincere in seeking God. We must belong to God alone, as a husband and wife belong to each other.

- How do you think about God? Do you belong only to him? Are you faithful to God? Or do you have other gods too? Do you need to turn away from your sin and turn back to God?

⊙ **Pray:** *Ask God to help you be faithful to him alone.*

⬇ STUDY: Deuteronomy 4:32-40

10 THERE IS NO OTHER GOD

❂ Background
Moses is preaching to Israel before they enter the promised land. Moses wants the people to learn from the past years in the desert. He wants the people to live good lives in the promised land.

⊙ Read verses 32-40.
Read each verse and explain it to yourself in your own words.

❂ Notes
- **Deuteronomy 4:32.** "Ask now about…" First, the people ask about time or history. Never before has anything so great as this happened. Second, the people ask about place ("from one end of heaven to another" (NIV)). Nowhere has anything so great as this happened.
- **Deuteronomy 4:35.** "Besides him there is no other" (NIV). No other god is as great as the Lord.
- **Deuteronomy 4:36.** "From heaven … on earth…" God is Lord of heaven and earth.
- **Deuteronomy 4:37.** "Forefathers" (NIV) or "ancestors" (GN) means Abraham, Isaac and Jacob.

⊙ Something to work on
- *In what ways is God greater than other gods?*

Deuteronomy 4:32-34 has questions. The answer to each question is **No**. No other people heard God speaking as the people of Israel did at Mount Sinai. No other god brought a nation out from another nation with signs and wonders as God did in Exodus. He brought the people of Israel out from Egypt.

Verse 35 tells us what to do. No other god can do what the Lord did. So do not worship other idols and gods. This verse reminds us of the first commandment in Deuteronomy 5:7.

Moses wants the people to know that the Lord is the greatest. Moses says this again in verses 36-39. God spoke from heaven. On earth, the people heard God's voice. God brought fire at Mount Sinai. On earth, God also brought the people of Israel out from Egypt.

The reason God brought the people of Israel out from Egypt was to bring them into the promised land. God's power defeated Egypt. God is strong to defeat the nations in the land.

⊕ MAIN POINT
There is no other god except the true God.

→ TEACH: Deuteronomy 4:32-40

⌄ Start

Sometimes people discuss who is the greatest footballer, or who is the greatest actor or who is the greatest leader. Deuteronomy 4:32-35 asks us to think: Who is the greatest God?

Who is the greatest?
⌄ **Read: *Deuteronomy 4:32-35***

Two things show the LORD is the greatest.

1. The LORD spoke out of the fire to the people. That happened at Mount Sinai.
2. The LORD took the people out from another nation. That happened in the exodus.

Tell your listeners the questions in verses 32-34 have the answer "No". No other God spoke to a nation out of fire. No other God took his people out from another nation. Such things never happened in any other time or place.

So who is the greatest? The LORD. There is no other like him (v35). The LORD is the best. The LORD speaks. The LORD is the strongest.

Again: Who is the greatest?
⌄ **Read: *Deuteronomy 4:36-39***

God is the greatest. This is so important that Moses repeats the point.

God spoke from heaven. God acted on earth. God is Lord of heaven and earth. The people of Israel heard his voice. God defeated Egypt with strength.

Verse 39 is like verse 35. The LORD is God. There is no other.

Trust and obey
⌄ **Read: *Deuteronomy 4:38, 40***

The people of Israel must learn two things.

1. Because God defeated Egypt with strength, the people can trust him to defeat the nations in the promised land.
2. Because God is the only God, obey his laws. Then the people will live long in the land.

Christians must still trust and obey God. We must trust God is powerful to save us from our sin. He showed his power on the cross. Jesus' death is powerful. We also must still obey him. We must live under his commands to us.

If someone suggests we follow another god or spirit, stop! The LORD is the greatest! If we think other gods are better, stop! The LORD is the greatest. If we think we do not need to obey God's laws, stop! God is the greatest. We must follow him alone.

⇡ **Pray:** *Ask God to help you trust and obey him fully in your life each day.*

STUDY: Deuteronomy 5:6-11

11 PUT GOD FIRST

Background
Deuteronomy 1 – 4 was about learning from the past. Deuteronomy 5 – 26 is laws from God. Moses begins with the Ten Commandments.

Read verses 6-11.

Notes
- **Deuteronomy 5:7.** God wants people to worship only him.
- **Deuteronomy 5:8.** The people of God must not make idols or images. God has no physical form. Look again at Deuteronomy 4:9-20. The people of Israel did not see God at Mount Sinai.
- **Deuteronomy 5:9-10.** "A jealous God" (NIV). Read Deuteronomy 4:3. God punishes guilty parents and children who make idols. "Punishing the children." This means children who do the same sin as their parents, not innocent children. "Third or fourth generation … thousand generations" (NIV). God's love lasts for ever. God's punishment lasts only a short time.
- **Deuteronomy 5:11.** "Misuse" means use in the wrong way. We must use God's name the right way.

Something to work on
The laws begin with the Ten Commandments. These commandments are the most important laws from God. God spoke them to all the people. God wrote them on stone tablets. The Ten Commandments are a summary of all the laws.

- *Why must the people obey these commandments?*

It is important that people obey God for the right reasons. Verse 6 says the people of Israel already belong to God. God saved them from Egypt. The people of God obey God's laws because they are his saved people. Obedience shows that we have a relationship with God.

The first three commandments are about relationship with God. God's people must not have other gods. God comes first because of what he did. God spoke to the people of Israel at Mount Sinai. God rescued the people from Egypt.

MAIN POINT
Worship God alone because he saved us.

→ TEACH: Deuteronomy 5:6-11

Why obey God?
⊙ Read: *Deuteronomy 5:6*
- Why should people obey God?

There are many reasons people have.
- Because they are afraid of God
- Because they want to be loved by God

The main reason is God already saved his people. In the Old Testament, God saved the Israelites from Egypt. Through Jesus on the cross God saved all believers from sin.

Our response is to obey him. *Explain to your listeners the importance of verse 6.*

The first three commandments are about a right relationship with God.

Put God first: No other gods
⊙ Read: *Deuteronomy 5:7*
We cannot worship God plus other gods. *Tell your listeners the reason for this commandment from Deuteronomy 4:32-40.* The LORD alone saved Israel from Egypt and spoke to the people at Mount Sinai.

Give some examples of other gods in your culture. They may be gods of other religions, or the god of money or the god of pleasure. If your culture has many gods, it is easy for people to try to worship God and other gods together.

Put God first: No idols
⊙ Read: *Deuteronomy 5:8-10*
We must not worship God using a statue or image or idol. *Tell your listeners the reason for this from Deuteronomy 4:9-20.* We cannot make a form of god to worship.

- Does your culture have idols? Are Christians tempted to have statues or images of God?

Put God first: Do not misuse God's name
⊙ Read: *Deuteronomy 5:11*
Explain to your listeners the meaning of "misuse". We must not say wrong things about God. We must not use the name of God for swearing. We must not use the name of God in sorcery. Do people in your place use the name of Jesus when they get angry? Christians must never do this.

Remember what God did for us. God saved us from sin through Jesus. So we must put God first in our life and worship. We must not worship another god. We must not have idols and statues. We must not use God's name in a wrong way. We will be thankful and we will love God.

⇡ **Pray:** *Ask God to help you put him first and never use his name in a wrong way.*

⬇ STUDY: Deuteronomy 5:12-15

12 KEEP GOD'S SABBATH

❨ Background
Moses is reminding the people of Israel of the Ten Commandments. The Sabbath commandment is the fourth commandment.

⊙ Read verses 12-15.
Read the passage 2 or 3 times.

❩ Notes
- **Deuteronomy 5:14.** The "seventh" day began at sunset on Friday and ended at sunset on Saturday.

- **Deuteronomy 5:14.** "Aliens" (NIV) are foreigners who choose to belong to the people of Israel.

⊙ Something to work on
The Sabbath day was the seventh day of the week. Read Genesis 2:1-3. God rested on the seventh day after the creation.

People must work for six days (v13). Some people are lazy. Maybe they do not work much. Some people work all the time. Maybe they work too much. People need one day a week without working.
- *Why do some people work too hard and why are some people lazy?*

Verses 12-14. The Sabbath day was a holy day. The day belonged to God. This law was for all God's people, even servants and aliens in Israel.

The reason for this law is in verse 15. As slaves in Egypt the people worked every day. They worked all the time. God brought them out of Egypt. Now they must give one day for rest and worship of God. Read Exodus 20:8-11. Another reason for the Sabbath law is that God created the world in six days and rested on the seventh day.

Jesus said that people can come to him and find rest (Matthew 11:28). Hebrews 4:9-11 speaks of a heavenly rest. Heaven will be an everlasting Sabbath with God. This is what the Sabbath day points forward to.

- *Do Christians have to keep a Sabbath day?*

Christians do not agree on this. Most Christians say that we need one day a week for rest and worship. Usually that is Sunday. Some Christians work on Sundays, like pastors. They need a different day of rest.

⊕ MAIN POINT
Keep a Sabbath day.

⊕ TEACH: Deuteronomy 5:12-15

⊙ Start
Imagine two people. One person is lazy and never works hard. The other person works every day. *Tell your listeners that the Sabbath day commandment speaks both to lazy people and people who work too hard. Ask your listeners to think if they are lazy or if they work too hard.*

What the Old Testament law said
⊙ **Read:** *Deuteronomy 5:12-15*
Explain to your listeners the reason from verse 15 to keep the Sabbath day. The Sabbath day was a joyful day. It celebrated the rescue by God of his people. All of the people, including servants and aliens, must keep the Sabbath day to remember what God did for them. It was a day for worship and rest with God. The day was different because God rested on the seventh day (Exodus 20:11). The law also said God's people must work for six days.

Do Christians still keep a Sabbath?
Help your listeners understand what this Old Testament law says to Christians. In the New Testament, there is no command for Christians to keep the Sabbath day.

The principle of the Sabbath day is one day each week for rest and worship. Christians must keep that principle, but the day can be any day of the week. We must not make extra laws about what people can do or cannot do on that day.

A greater Sabbath
Jesus invited people to come to him for rest. The best rest is with Jesus. One day this will be rest in heaven.

Each week we must have a day of rest and worship. That day is like a taste of heaven. Make sure you spend that day in rest, worship and spending time with God.

The law also says people must work six days. God wants us to work well. *Encourage your listeners who are lazy to become hard workers.*

⊕ **Apply:** Many of us work too hard. We give all our time to our work. Some may give an excuse that they must work to provide enough money for their family. God says we must rest one day a week.
When we work every day, we do not honour God. God will give us all we need. A rest day shows we trust God.

⊕ **Pray:** *Give thanks for a day each week to worship and rest.*

STUDY: Deuteronomy 5:16-21

13 LOVE OTHER PEOPLE

Background
Moses prepares the people to live in the promised land. Moses reminds the people of the Ten Commandments.

Read verses 16-21.

Notes
- **Deuteronomy 5:16.** "Honour" (NIV) means respect. This command is both for little children and adults.

- **Deuteronomy 5:17.** "Murder" does not include accidents. It does not include killing very bad criminals. It does not include killing in some wars.

- **Deuteronomy 5:18.** "Commit adultery." This means having sex outside marriage.

- **Deuteronomy 5:21.** "Covet" (NIV) is to desire strongly something that belongs to another person.

Something to work on
Remember: The people of God must obey these commandments because they saw what God is like (Deuteronomy 5:6). God brought them out from Egypt. For Christians also, we obey God, who saved us by the cross of Jesus.

- What should Christians do if their parents command them not to worship God. How does the child honour their parents (v16) but obey God?

Verses 17-18. God's people must respect human life. People are made in the image of God (Genesis 1:26). God's people must also be faithful to love their husband or wife. Sex is for people married to each other.

Verse 19. To steal another person's things is wrong. This includes cheating in our jobs, and stealing money or time from the government or our employer.

Verse 20. God's people must speak the truth. We must not lie. We must not mislead or trick people. We must be like this when we give evidence in court, and also in our talk with other people.

Verse 21. To covet shows our greed for things that belong to other people. When we strongly desire other things, it means we are not happy with what we have.

We must put God first. We must be happy with what God gives us. We must not be greedy or selfish in our relationships with other people.

MAIN POINT
Put God first by loving other people.

◉ TEACH: Deuteronomy 5:16-21

◉ Start

Many people know the Ten Commandments. But it is hard to obey them. All ten commandments are about putting God first. The people of God must keep these commandments because God rescued them from Egypt.

Loving other people

◉ **Read:** *Deuteronomy 5:16-21*

We put God first by loving other people. The people of God must honour parents, respect them and obey good commands (v16). But if parents command bad things, like disobeying God, God's people should disobey their parents and obey God.

• **Murder is wrong (v17).** Humans are made in the image of God. We must not murder other people. Most murder is from being selfish and greedy.

• **Sex outside marriage is wrong (v18).** Husbands and wives must be faithful to each other. God made sex for married couples to enjoy.

• **To steal another person's things is greedy and selfish (v19).**

⊕ **Illustration:** A man changes the church or company accounts so he can take some money. Another man keeps some things that belong to others. He pretends they were lost. Another man takes food that belongs to someone else. All these men steal. God's people should be thankful for what God gives them.

• **The truth is important (v20).** We must not lie for any reason. Our words must always be true. When we lie, we break down trust and relationships. More important, we disobey God.

⊕ **Illustration:** A man does not want to feel shame with his customer. He makes up an excuse for the customer. He lied. To speak the truth is brave but it is always the right thing to do. With our family, we must also speak the truth. A father does not want to go into the town with his children. So he tells them he is not going. Then he goes in secret. That is lying.

• **We must not be greedy for other people's things.** Greed comes from wrong hearts (v21). Do you want the clothes or new house belonging to someone else? That is greedy and wrong.

These commandments are for every Christian today. The people of God will want to obey them because God has rescued them by the cross.

⊕ **Pray:** *Ask God to help you tell the truth, not be greedy, and love other people.*

STUDY: Deuteronomy 6:4-9

14 LOVE GOD WITH ALL YOUR HEART

◉ Background
Moses reminds the people of God's commandments. He summarises the commandments as one great commandment.

◉ Read verses 4-9.
Read the passage 2 or 3 times. Read each verse and explain it to yourself in your own words.

◉ Notes
- **Deuteronomy 6:4.** "The Lord is one" (NIV) means the Lord alone is God. See also Deuteronomy 4:35.

- **Deuteronomy 6:5.** "Heart" means your decisions, thinking and feeling. "Soul" means all your life. "Strength" means effort and possessions.

- **Deuteronomy 6:7.** "At home … along the road/away" means in any place. "Lie down … get up" (NIV) means at any time.

- **Deuteronomy 6:8.** "Hands" (NIV) or "arms" (GN) means everything we do must obey God. "Foreheads" means everything we think must obey God.

◉ Something to work on
Verse 4 means that only the Lord is God. There is no other God for the people of Israel. There is no other God. The people of Israel must not worship other gods.

The main command is verse 5. The focus is on "all". The people must love God with all they are and all they have. The right response to God is love. Love is loyal, faithful and lasts for a long time. Love shows in action. Love is not just a feeling. The people of God must have a close relationship with God.

To obey God comes from a loving heart. So the commandments must be in the hearts of the people (v6). This is why the Bible tells us to read and think about the law (or word) of God every day (Psalm 1:2).

- *How do we get the word of God into our hearts?*

Verses 7-9. Parents must teach their children about God's word. This must be done everywhere and all the time. This shows how important God's commandments are. Verse 8 means that everything the people do and think must obey God. Verse 9 means that our homes must obey God.

⊕ MAIN POINT
Love God with all your heart.

→ TEACH: Deuteronomy 6:4-9

⊙ Start
A man asked Jesus: "What is the greatest commandment?" Jesus said: "Love the Lord your God with all your heart." Jesus quoted Deuteronomy 6:5. This commandment is very important.

The Lord alone is God
⊙ **Read: *Deuteronomy 6:4***
Moses already said that the Lord alone is God. There is no other (Deuteronomy 4:35). Only the Lord is God for the people of Israel. No other god is real.

Love God with all your heart
⊙ **Read: *Deuteronomy 6:5-6***
If the Lord alone is God, then the people must love him with all their hearts, souls and strength. *Tell your listeners what heart, soul and strength mean.* God wants all our love.

Love is the main thing. We must obey God from love. Love is not only a feeling. Love shows in action. We cannot say we love God when we disobey his commandments.

- How much of you loves God? We must put God's commandments in our hearts (v6) so that we love God with all our hearts (v5).

How do we make our hearts love God?
⊙ **Read: *Deuteronomy 6:7-9***

To put God's commandments in our hearts we must:

- **Teach them** always to our children (v7).
- **Remind ourselves** that what we do and think must be right (v8).
- **Remind ourselves** of God's commandments when we enter and leave our homes (v9).

We must remember God's commandments all the time. This is so the commandments will go deep into our hearts and lives. If we really love God, then we will love his commandments, and read them often, and follow them in our lives.

Christians are not the same as the people of Israel. Christians have the Holy Spirit to write God's word in their hearts. The Spirit does this when we think about and read God's commandments often.

✣ **Illustration:** Some people wear a band on their wrist that has the letters WWJD. These letters stand for: "What would Jesus do?" People wear this band as a reminder to obey and love God.

Ask your listeners: What will they do to remember God's commandments more? What will they do to love God more?

↑ **Pray:** *Ask God to help you to love him and obey him all the time.*

STUDY: Deuteronomy 6:20-25

15 TEACH YOUR CHILDREN

Background
Moses prepares the people of Israel to enter and live in the promised land. He tells the people to teach their children what God did in the past and why they must obey the commandments of God.

Read verses 20-25.

Notes
- **Deuteronomy 6:21-22.** This is about the exodus. See Exodus 7 – 14.
- **Deuteronomy 6:23.** "Forefathers" (NIV) or "ancestors" (GN) are Abraham, Isaac and Jacob. God promised the land first to Abraham in Genesis 12:7.
- **Deuteronomy 6:24.** "Prosper" (NIV) means to do well.
- **Deuteronomy 6:25.** "Righteousness" (NIV) means to be right with God.

Something to work on
"What is the meaning of the laws?" Moses thinks of a child who asks his parents this question one day.

Why will the child obey God's law? The reason is God brought the people of Israel out from Egypt and brought them into the promised land. The answer focuses on God's grace. God's grace must lead them to obey God's law and to "fear" God. To fear God is like having faith.

Why should the people of Israel obey God's laws? Because they are God's people already. God rescued them. God brought them into the promised land. The law is a guide to living for those who are saved.

Israelites who obey God's laws will be righteous. They obey "before the LORD", meaning they already have a relationship with God. They fear him. Abraham was righteous before God through faith (Genesis 15:6). But his faith and actions worked together (James 2:22). (Look again at Study 3 to see that disobedience and lack of faith go together.) An Israelite who is right with God will have faith that is seen in obedience.

The reason to obey God is important. A wrong reason is to try to get God's acceptance. The right reason is to respond to God's grace. Faith is shown in obedience.

It is important to teach this to our children. We must teach them how to obey God. Even more, we must teach them the gospel of God's grace to encourage obedience.

MAIN POINT
We obey God to please him, because he has saved us.

➲ TEACH: Deuteronomy 6:20-25

◉ Start
Children often complain to their parents. "Why must I be clean?" "Why cannot I play with my friends?" "Why must I chop wood and do work?" Some parents may say: "Because I tell you."
- Why must God's people obey God's laws?

The question
◉ Read: *Deuteronomy 6:20*
Moses thinks of a child who asks his parents a question. "What is the meaning of the laws?" The question means: "Why must we obey?" Moses wants to make sure every generation knows the answer and obeys God's laws.

The answer
◉ Read: *Deuteronomy 6:21-25*
The answer is in three parts.

1. God rescued his people from Egypt (v21-22). *Tell your listeners about the story of the exodus.* The people must obey the law because God rescued them. God gave the people laws so they could live for him and put him first.

2. So that the people will do well in the promised land (v23-24). God wants the people to prosper and do well in the land.

3. The people will be righteous if they obey. *Explain to your listeners that righteousness means to be right with God. God will be pleased with them. Abraham was righteous by faith, seen in obedience.* The people must obey from faith.

◉ **Apply:** Parents must tell children what God has done. Parents must tell children how to obey, to live as God's people. Parents must explain the reasons for obeying God with faith. *Challenge the parents about what they do to teach their children about God.*

Jesus died to rescue believers from sin. That is why Christians want to obey God and put God first in everything. We are made right through faith in Jesus. We show faith by obeying God.

Because all people sin, God sent Jesus. We are righteous because of Jesus' death. We must still live lives of faith, seen in obedience. Praise God for what is ahead for all who truly follow Jesus. Teach your children about it.

◉ **Pray:** *Ask God to help you remember what Jesus did for you on the cross so you will obey and love him more.*

STUDY: Deuteronomy 7:1-11

16 CHOSEN TO BE HOLY

Background
Moses prepares the people to enter and live in the promised land. The big problem is the nations who live in the land. These nations worship other gods. Moses warns the people not to worship the pagan gods.

Read verses 1-11.
Read the passage 2 or 3 times.

Notes
- **Deuteronomy 7:1.** These seven nations all lived in the promised land.
- **Deuteronomy 7:2.** "Destroy them totally" (NIV). Not one of the enemy nations is to stay alive.
- **Deuteronomy 7:5.** "Asherah poles" (NIV) are tall wooden poles used to worship fake pagan gods.
- **Deuteronomy 7:6.** "Treasured possession" (NIV) is someone's most precious belonging. The people of Israel are God's most precious belonging.
- **Deuteronomy 7:7.** "You were the fewest/smallest" refers to Abraham and Sarah, only two people.

Something to work on
Verse 1. The nations are stronger than Israel. But God is stronger than the nations. So the people of Israel will win.

Verses 2-5. The main problem is not that these nations are stronger. The main problem is their fake gods. The gods of the nations are a danger or temptation for the people of Israel. So the people of Israel must totally destroy the people from the other nations. They must not marry any of those people. They must destroy the pagan places of worship and idols.

Verse 6. Israel must be different. They must not have idols and other gods. They must put God first. This is what being holy means. The people of Israel are chosen by God. They are his special possession. The people of Israel are loved by God.

Verses 7-11. Why does God love the people of Israel? Because he keeps his promise to Abraham. The people of Israel are the descendants of Abraham. They are rescued from Egypt. Therefore they must behave differently from other nations.

- *How will a relationship with God change the way we behave?*

⊕ MAIN POINT
Christians are a people holy to God.

→ TEACH: Deuteronomy 7:1-11

⊙ Start
It is easy to be led to do bad things by people around us. For example, children and youth can follow bad examples at school like swearing or using drugs. Adults can follow bad examples at work, such as cheating or drinking alcohol. *Give ideas to your listeners of some bad examples in your place.*

Bad examples
⊙ **Read: *Deuteronomy 7:1-5***
The people of Israel were about to enter the promised land. The nations in the land worshipped other gods. So God's people had to destroy the nations and their places of worship. This was because those nations would be a bad example for the people of God.

The people of Israel must destroy the idols and altars of the pagans. These things could tempt them to wrong worship. Sometimes we think we are strong to fight temptation. But people are often weak. We must run away from temptation. So the people of Israel must remove the idols. Then they will not be tempted.

Why God's people are different
⊙ **Read: *Deuteronomy 7:6-8***
Explain to your listeners why God chose the people of Israel.

Sometimes we think that "holy" is about special saints. But all God's people are holy. It means we belong to God. This comes from God choosing us to belong to him.

⊙ **Apply:** *Challenge your listeners: Do they really belong to God? Are they holy? Do they put God first in their lives? Do they behave in a different way from unbelievers?*

⊕ **Illustration:** An unbeliever was travelling in another country. Every time he met Christians he saw that they behaved differently. They were honest. They were loving. They were different. They helped him when he lost his wallet. They cared for him when he was sick.

Be different
⊙ **Read: *Deuteronomy 7:9-11***
God is faithful. God still loves his people. The command in verse 11 talks about the whole passage. Follow the commands of God, because God's people are holy, because God's people are different, because God's people are chosen and loved by God. So God's people must obey God and follow his laws.

- Think about your life. What will unbelievers say about how you live?

⊙ **Pray:** *Ask God to give strength for his people to be different from unbelievers.*

STUDY: Deuteronomy 8:1-20

17 BE HUMBLE, NOT PROUD

Background
The people have been in the desert for nearly forty years. God tested the people in the desert. The desert was a hard and dry place. It was not easy to live there. The promised land will be very different.

Read verses 1-20.

Notes
- **Deuteronomy 8:3.** "Manna" was the special food from God. The word "manna" means "What is it?" Nobody knows what it was.

- **Deuteronomy 8:12.** "Satisfied" (NIV). The people will have everything they want.

- **Deuteronomy 8:17.** "Say to yourself" (NIV). The original words are: "Say in your heart".

Something to work on
Read chapter 8 and notice the words "remember" and "forget", "humble" and "proud". These words are important for this chapter.

Verses 1-6. The forty years in the desert were a test from God. God made the Israelites hungry and he fed them strange food. God first gave the manna in Exodus 16. It went bad during the night, except for the night before the Sabbath day. This was a miracle from God to make the people humble.

Verses 7-10. The desert did not have much food. The land will have lots of food.

Verses 11-14. After some time in the land, the things the people have will increase. They will be satisfied. But the danger is pride. Proud people do not rely on God.

Verses 15-18. Moses tells the people to remember the desert so they will not be proud in the land. The words of verse 17 come from proud hearts. "Wealth/wealthy" means riches/rich.

Verses 19-20. Being proud leads to idolatry, the worship of other gods. Moses warns the people not to worship other gods.

- *Why are the hearts of people so proud? If you understand why hearts are proud, your sermon will be more powerful. Does being proud come more from hard times, like the desert, or from easy times, like the promised land?*

⊕ MAIN POINT
Remember how God humbled you. Keep humble and rely on him.

➜ TEACH: Deuteronomy 8:1-20

⊞ Illustration: A man's wife dies and he has no job. He is angry and complains to God. He loses his faith. A woman finds her life is good. She gets more things and is rich. But then she moves away from God.
- Do bad times or good times lead people away from God?

Remember the test in the desert
⊙ Read: *Deuteronomy 8:1-6*
Moses reminds the people of Israel about living in the desert for forty years. *Explain to your listeners how God humbled Israel by making them hungry and then feeding them with manna.* That is what being humble is about. It is about depending on God. The people of Israel must remember and not forget the past.

The promised land is very different
⊙ Read: *Deuteronomy 8:7-11*
The promised land is very different from the desert. The promised land is full of good things—rivers of water, plenty of crops, much fruit, copper. At first, the people will thank God (v10).

The promised land is also a test
⊙ Read: *Deuteronomy 8:12-18*
In the promised land, the people of Israel will get more things: animals, silver and gold. They will be full. But this is a danger. If the people forget God and forget what God did, they will become proud. They will think they became rich because of themselves and not because of God.

The desert was a test to make the people of Israel humble. In the promised land, they must still be humble. Being proud is a common sin. A proud person thinks he does not need to rely on God. A proud person thinks he is able to get what he needs by himself (v17). So watch out! Are you proud?

Danger of idolatry
⊙ Read: *Deuteronomy 8:19-20*
If the people are proud, they will then worship other gods. They will not trust the true God. Moses warns the people strongly against idol worship.

⊙ Apply: God's people must always rely on God. We must make sure we are humble. Remember what God did in the desert for the people of Israel. Remember what God did for you through the cross of Jesus—how he provided for you and helped you.

⊙ Pray: *Ask God to help you see your pride. Thank God for everything he gives you.*

STUDY: Deuteronomy 9:4-24

18 REMEMBER HOW YOU FAILED

⊙ Read verses 4-24.
Read the passage 2 or 3 times.

⊛ Notes
- **Deuteronomy 9:4.** "Righteous" (NIV) mostly means to be right with God. In this verse it means "good".

- **Deuteronomy 9:6** "Stiff-necked" (NIV) is to be stubborn, like an ox or donkey that does not go where you want.

- **Deuteronomy 9:9.** "Tablets of the covenant" (NIV). The Ten Commandments were written by God on two stones. "Covenant" means a strong, binding relationship, like a marriage.

- **Deuteronomy 9:18.** "Prostrate" (NIV) is to lie face down on the ground.

⊙ Something to work on
Moses reminds the Israelites of their rebellion at Mount Sinai when the people made a golden calf to worship.

- *Why does God give the people of Israel the land?*

Verses 4-6. When God gives the people the promised land, the people may think they are better than the other nations. They may think the land is a reward from God. So Moses tells the people they are not more righteous than the other nations. The land is a gift from God. The people are stubborn (stiff-necked). They refuse to obey God.

Verses 7, 22-24. The people always rebel against God. In Exodus and Numbers, the Israelites always complained and turned against God. Moses gives a summary here. To rebel against God is to disobey and not trust God. The people do not deserve the promised land.

Verses 8-17. The people's biggest sin was to make a gold calf (baby cow) to worship. Read Exodus 32 – 34 for the full story. The people disobeyed the first two of the Ten Commandments. That was very bad and rude to God, who brought them out from Egypt.

God was angry with the people of Israel. God wanted to destroy them. Moses broke the two stone tablets. This was like tearing up a written agreement, or even like tearing up a wedding certificate. It was a sign that God wanted to finish the relationship with his people. He wanted to end the covenant.

⊕ MAIN POINT
Never forget that you are a sinner.

→ TEACH: Deuteronomy 9:4-24

⊙ Start
It is easy to think we deserve God. Deserve means we earned something or have a right to it. We can think: "I am better than that other person". "I deserve to go to heaven because I am good."
• Do you sometimes think like that?

The people do not deserve the land
⊙ **Read:** *Deuteronomy 9:4-6*
When the Israelites enter the land, they may think they are better than other nations. They may think they deserve the land. Moses tells them they do not. The people of Israel are stubborn (stiff-necked).

⊕ **Illustration:** Maybe you have an animal on your farm for ploughing the land. If the animal disobeys you, it makes its neck stiff and hard. That is what the people of Israel were like.

The people always rebel against God
⊙ **Read:** *Deuteronomy 9:7, 22-24*
After the people left Egypt, they complained about food, water, their leaders and the desert many times.

The people's biggest sin was idol worship
⊙ **Read:** *Deuteronomy 9:8-21*
The people's biggest sin was to make an idol at Mount Sinai. The idol was made of gold and looked like a baby cow. God was very angry and decided to destroy his people. Making an idol is like spiritual adultery. That is why God was so angry. That is why Moses broke the stone tablets that had the Ten Commandments written on them.

⊕ **Illustration:** Imagine it is your wedding day. At the end of the day, you go to your room for the night. Your husband or wife is already there. You are excited and happy. When you open the door, you see your new husband or wife in bed with another person. You are very angry. You tear up your marriage papers. The relationship is ended.

① **Apply:** The people of Israel did not deserve to enter the land. But later God gave the people of Israel the land because of grace. We do not deserve to enter heaven. Remember how we rebelled against God in the past. We deserve hell. God gives us the right to enter heaven only by his grace in Jesus. We must never think we deserve to go to heaven.

↑ **Pray:** *Ask God to help you remember there is nothing special about you. Thank God for his grace and forgiveness.*

STUDY: Deuteronomy 9:25-29

19 HOW TO PRAY FOR OTHERS

◉ Background
Moses reminds the people of their sin—making an idol at Mount Sinai. God wanted to destroy the people. Moses prayed for the people.

◉ Read verses 25-29.
Read the passage 2 or 3 times.

◉ Notes
• Deuteronomy 9:26. "Inheritance" (NIV) here means the people are like God's children. "Redeem" (NIV) means to rescue, to buy from slavery.

◉ Something to work on
• *How serious are you about prayer for your people when they are disobedient and stubborn?*

This passage is a big challenge for leaders as we see how Moses prayed for the people.

Moses lay on the ground for forty days and nights before God (v18, 25). He fasted and prayed.

In verse 12, God said he will destroy the people because of their sin. Moses asked God not to destroy the people of Israel. There were **three reasons** Moses gave to God not to destroy them.
• *Can you find them before you read on?*

Verse 26. *First reason:* The people belong to God. God redeemed (bought) and rescued the people from Egypt. The people are God's inheritance. If God destroys the people, then what God did to redeem them is wasted.

Verse 27. *Second reason:* Remember Abraham, Isaac and Jacob. In Genesis 12:1-7, God promised Abraham the land and many descendants. If God destroys the people, God's promises to Abraham will be broken. Moses asks God to keep his promises.

Verse 28. *Third reason:* The people of Egypt will think wrong things about God. God wants his name to be honoured by the nations. If God destroys the people, the Egyptians will think God is weak or hates the people of Israel. His purpose will fail.

How do you pray for sinful believers? This prayer is a wonderful example of prayer for forgiveness. There is no excuse for Israel's sin. The prayer focuses on God's faithfulness and purposes. What about your prayers? God answers Moses' prayer (see Deuteronomy 9:19 and 10:1-5).

⊕ MAIN POINT
Pray for God to forgive others.

➔ TEACH: Deuteronomy 9:25-29

⊙ Start
- How much do you pray for believers who sin?

God wants to destroy the people of Israel after they make an idol. But Moses prays. He gives us an example of how to pray seriously for believers who sin. He prayed face down for forty days and nights without eating! Moses gives three reasons why God should not destroy Israel.

God has rescued the people
⊙ Read: *Deuteronomy 9:26, 29*

Moses reminds God that the people belong to him. They are his children. God has redeemed them already. The rescue from Egypt will be for nothing if God destroys the people now.

God made promises
⊙ Read: *Deuteronomy 9:27*

Moses reminds God of the promises God made to Abraham, Isaac and Jacob. God promised land and descendants. The promises will be nothing if God destroys the people.

Other nations will not honour God
⊙ Read: *Deuteronomy 9:28*

Moses says the people of Egypt will think God cannot bring the people of Israel into the land, or God hates the people of Israel. God wants the nations to honour him. Moses does not want the nations to think wrong things about God.

What lessons are there for believers today? When we pray for people who sin, we can use the three reasons in Moses' prayer.

1. **"Because of Jesus who died for me"**: God saved his people by Jesus' death, like the rescue of the people of Israel.
2. **"Remember your promises"**: God promises that sinful people are saved through Jesus' death.
3. **"For the good of unbelievers"**: When believers sin and God punishes them, unbelievers may think God is weak. God's name will be dishonoured and unbelievers will not want to follow God.

- Are there believers you know who have sinned? Will you be serious to pray for them that God will bring them back?

God listened and agreed to what Moses asked. God gave two more stone tablets with the Ten Commandments (Deuteronomy 10:1-5). The special relationship between God and Israel was made right. What a forgiving God!

⇧ **Pray**: *Ask God for forgiveness for Christians who have sinned, so that Jesus' death is not wasted for them, so that God's faithfulness is seen and so that other people will not dishonour God's name.*

STUDY: Deuteronomy 10:12-22

20 WHAT DOES GOD ASK FOR?

Background
Moses prepares the people to live in the promised land. He summarises what God wants from his people.

Read verses 1-8.

Notes
- **Deuteronomy 10:12.** "Fear" (NIV) or "revere" means to respect and honour. God is an awesome God. We respect or fear him.

- **Deuteronomy 10:13.** "Observe" (NIV) is to obey God's commands.

- **Deuteronomy 10:16.** "Circumcise" (NIV). See Study 35. In Genesis 17, Abraham physically circumcised himself and his family. But true circumcision is of the heart (Romans 2:28-29). God promises he will circumcise people's hearts in the future to make them obey and love him (Deuteronomy 30:6).

- **Deuteronomy 10:17.** "Shows no partiality" means God treats everyone as equals.

- **Deuteronomy 10:18.** An "alien" (NIV) is a foreigner who wants to live always in Israel.

Something to work on
Verses 12-13. God asks for five things from his people. Think about what each one means in practice.

1. **Fear God:** This does not mean to be afraid of God. It means God is holy and powerful. We treat him with care.
2. **Walk in his ways:** This means that every day we obey what God says.
3. **Love God:** This is from the heart. It means we put God first.
4. **Serve God:** This includes worship of God, alone or with others.
5. **Observe God's commandments:** This means to obey God's laws.

Verses 14-15. Why do God's people do these five things? Because of who God is. He is the great Maker but he also loves his people.

Verse 16. The people need a change in their hearts to do what God asks for. Their hearts are stubborn and proud.

Verses 17-19. God loves people in need. God also wants his people to love others in need, like the fatherless, widows and aliens.

Verses 20-22. Again, God's people must fear God and serve him. They must praise God because he brought his people from Egypt.

MAIN POINT
Fear, love and serve the Lord.

→ TEACH: Deuteronomy 10:12-22

⊙ Start
- What does God ask from his people? What is the most important thing?

What does God ask for?
⊙ **Read: *Deuteronomy 10:12-13***
These verses tell us the most important things. *Tell your listeners what each of the five things is. Give some examples of how to do them.*

Why does God want this?
⊙ **Read: *Deuteronomy 10:14-15***
God wants our total devotion because he is a great God and his people are special to him. He chose them to be his. God loves his people. God wants his people to love and obey him in their hearts.

The problem
⊙ **Read: *Deuteronomy 10:16***
Explain to your listeners how God told Abraham to circumcise his family. This was a physical sign to show they belonged to God for ever (Genesis 17:13). But the real problem is in the human heart. We need God to change our hearts so that we do the five things. We cannot change ourselves.

Our hearts can only be changed by Jesus. When we believe in Jesus, his Spirit lives in our heart to change us from the inside. The Holy Spirit makes us more like Jesus.

Behave to others as God behaves to others
⊙ **Read: *Deuteronomy 10:17-19***
Explain what God is like from verse 17. He is far above any gods or powers. God is just and treats everyone equally. God loves people in need. He wants them to be treated justly and kindly. The fatherless and widows are often poor. Aliens do not own land. They may need help. God loves all these people. God wanted the people of Israel to love them too.

Serve and praise God
⊙ **Read: *Deuteronomy 10:20-22***
The passage finishes where it began—fear and serve God. God rescued the people of Israel from Egypt. So God's people must praise him.

① **Apply:** How well do you do what God asks for? Do you always put God first? Remember the five key things in verses 12-13. Do you love needy people?

The things in this passage are hard to do. How can we do what he wants? Jesus gives us his Spirit to help us and change our hearts.

① **Pray:** *Ask God for his help so you can do what he wants. Thank God for giving his Spirit to help all believers.*

STUDY: Deuteronomy 12:1-7

21 WORSHIP IN GOD'S WAY

⊗ Background
Moses prepares the people of Israel to live in the promised land. Now he gives many laws about all parts of life.

⊙ Read verses 1-7.
Read the passage 2 or 3 times. Read each verse and explain it to yourself in your own words.

⊗ Notes
• Deuteronomy 12:3. "Sacred stones." Special stones to represent male gods. Wooden "Asherah poles" (NIV) represented female gods.

• Deuteronomy 12:5. "To put his Name there." God will live among his people.

⊙ Something to work on
Verses 2-4. The people of Canaan often worshipped on hills and under big trees. Hills are close to the sky. Big trees were signs of life and fertility.

The people of Canaan believed their gods gave rain, crops, animals and children. They used wrong sex, and special stones and poles, to get these things.

The people of Israel must not use the same places or things for their own worship of the true God. They must keep away from temptation and destroy these things.

• *In your place, what are the wrong things that people worship (for example, magic practices and statues of other gods)? We may not be able to destroy them, but how can we keep away from them?*

Verse 5. This is an important verse. The LORD will choose one place in the whole land. The people of Israel do not choose the place.

Verses 6-7. At this place, the people must offer the right sacrifices and offerings (see Leviticus 1 – 7). "Eat" and "rejoice/enjoy" mean the people of Israel have much to thank God for. God blesses and gives. Other gods do not do that.

• *What does this say to Christians?* We do not go to a special place. Jesus said that the real temple is his risen body (John 2:21). Jesus is the name above every name. Christians must worship Jesus everywhere, not in one place. Jesus is where God meets his people.

⊕ MAIN POINT
Do not worship like people of other religions. Worship God in the way he says.

→ TEACH: Deuteronomy 12:1-7

> **Start:** Christians often disagree over how we worship together.
- What are the most important things about Christian worship?

Where God's people must not worship
⊙ **Read: *Deuteronomy 12:2-4***
Tell your listeners about the things used for pagan worship in the land, and how the people of Israel must destroy those places and things.

Talk about some of the wrong worship of other gods that happens in your place. Christians must not be tempted to worship God in the ways of other religions.

Where God's people must worship
⊙ **Read: *Deuteronomy 12:5***
God told the people of Israel he would choose a place for them to worship. Long after Moses, God chose Jerusalem. The temple was built there. God chose to live in the middle of the temple.

What does this tell Christians today? Jesus' risen body is the true temple. Read John 2:21. The Old Testament temple worship pointed to Jesus. After Jesus came, temple worship was no longer needed. Jesus was God living on earth among people. All Christians must worship Jesus. So Christians can worship in any place. Religions that do not worship Jesus are not true.

How God's people must worship
⊙ **Read: *Deuteronomy 12:6-7***
At the place God chooses, the Israelites must offer sacrifices and offerings. Some sacrifices were for sin. Others were to thank God. The people of Israel must eat and rejoice in the place God chooses. There is joy because of what God has done. These sacrifices all pointed forward to Jesus. Jesus was the true sacrifice. Christians do not offer animal sacrifices. Jesus is our sacrifice.

⊙ **Apply:** For Christians, we see in this passage:
- Worship is only possible because of Jesus.
- We come to God only through the sacrifice of Jesus on the cross.
- We do not worship in the ways of other religions and with idols.
- We have joy in worship because of what God has done for us in Jesus.
- We worship together as God's people, not only as individuals.

When you meet with God's people for worship, do you think about these things? Is Jesus who you worship?

⊕ **Pray:** *Ask God to help you worship Jesus, with joy, together with God's people.*

◉ **STUDY: Deuteronomy 13:1-11**

22 DO NOT LET ANYONE LEAD YOU AWAY FROM GOD

❂ Background
Moses is helping the people of Israel get ready to live in the promised land.

⊙ Read verses 1-11.
Read the passage 2 or 3 times. Read each verse and explain it to yourself in your own words.

❂ Notes
- **Deuteronomy 13:1-3.** Some false prophets have power to do miracles. Some share dreams.
- **Deuteronomy 13:5.** "Purge the evil" (NIV) means to take out the root of evil from the people.
- **Deuteronomy 13:6.** "Entices" (NIV) means to tempt or attract.

⊙ Something to work on
- *If someone can do a miracle, does that mean they are from God? If the miracle is a bad thing, like sickness or death, then the miracle is not from God. But what about a good miracle?*

Verses 1-5. A false prophet may be able to do a miracle. People can think this must be God's power. But a false prophet leads people to follow other gods. People may be confused. Moses says that the important thing is which god the prophet follows. The people must put the false prophet to death.

Verses 6-11. What if a family member invited you to worship other gods? People are often pressured by family members who they love. But if the family member led people to follow other gods, they must put the person to death.

The reason for punishment of death was to stop the sin spreading. When other people heard of the punishment, they were warned not to do the same sin. The people of Israel must live as a pure and holy nation. Serious sin must be punished.

⊙ Apply:
Christians must not put false prophets to death in our countries. **But we must not listen to them.** We must reject their teaching. If they do a miracle, or share their dreams, we must not follow other gods. We do not put the person to death. But they must not be a member of the church. Their bad teaching must not spread to others.

⊕ MAIN POINT
God's people must reject people who lead them away from God.

➔ TEACH: Deuteronomy 13:1-11

◉ Start
- If a person does a miracle, does this mean God is happy with that person?

Do not follow false prophets
◉ **Read: *Deuteronomy 13:1-5***
False prophets may do miracles and have dreams. The important thing is to check what every prophet or preacher teaches. Do they teach the truth?

✳ **Illustration:** A preacher came to a village one day and did some miracles. He spoke the name of Jesus. But the prophet said that he himself was Jesus returned. Many people followed him because of his miracles. But he was a false prophet. To use God's name does not mean the preacher is from God.

Do not follow family members who lead to other gods
◉ **Read: *Deuteronomy 13:6-11***
It is very hard if someone we love wants us to follow other gods. If we love someone, we want to agree with them.

God's people must love God with all their hearts. They must love God more than their family or friends. If a friend or family member tries to lead us to follow other gods, we must not listen to them.

✳ **Illustration:** A wife says to her husband that she has heard a new preacher who does great miracles. She very much wants her husband to come and hear the prophet. The husband says no. But the wife keeps asking her husband. Because he loves his wife, he gives in and goes. He is led the wrong way.

Christians must not put false teachers to death today. But we must not listen to false prophets. We must send them out of the church. They have no place among the people of God.

False teachers may be loved by many people—perhaps by family members or friends. But they are dangerous. God's people must know the difference between what is true and what is wrong.

- Do you test the words that people speak?
- Do you test the words of your preachers with God's word?

⬆ **Pray:** *Ask God to help his church be strong and wise to know the truth. Ask God to protect his church from false teachers.*

STUDY: Deuteronomy 14:1-21

23 GOD'S PEOPLE MUST BE HOLY

❂ Background
Moses is preparing the people of Israel to live in the promised land. God's people must live in a different way from the other nations.

⊙ Read verses 1-21.
Read the passage 2 or 3 times.

❂ Notes
- **Deuteronomy 14:2, 21.** "Holy" (NIV) means belonging to God. God's people do not belong to the world.
- **Deuteronomy 14:7.** "Unclean." The animal is not dirty, but God says his people must not eat it.

⊙ Something to work on
Verses 1-2, 21. The people of Israel are holy. They are God's children. They must live as God wants them to. Some people cut themselves as a way of being sad when someone died. At that time some pagans cooked a young goat in its mother's milk as a magic thing. God's people must not do these things.

Verses 3-8. Why was a cow clean but a pig was unclean? Why did God choose the people of Israel but not other nations (v2)? We do not know but God said this. Some animals were clean, like the people of Israel. Other animals were unclean, like the other nations. The people of Israel belonged to God so they must not eat unclean animals.

Verses 9-20. Some water animals, such as prawns and shellfish, and some birds and insects were unclean.

Christians do not have to keep these laws. Jesus said all foods are clean (Mark 7:19). Peter had a vision from God which also said all foods are clean (Acts 10:9-15). The reason for the change is because of Jesus. The gospel is now for everyone, Jew and Gentile. But God's people must still be different from unbelievers. Christians must be careful not to eat food that some people think makes them sin (1 Corinthians 8:4-13).

- *Are there wrong understandings about food in your place? Do some still follow Old Testament rules? How can you help them to be free in Christ?*

⊕ MAIN POINT
God's people must be different from unbelievers.

→ TEACH: Deuteronomy 14:1-21

⊙ Start
- What do you do if someone invites you to a religious meal of another religion? Here's another question. The Old Testament says not to eat pig. Do you have to obey this?

The food laws in Deuteronomy 14 are strange for many people. What do they teach us?

God's people Israel must only eat clean food
⊙ **Read: *Deuteronomy 14:3-20***
The people of Israel must only eat clean foods. A clean food was decided by God. It did not mean specially good or healthy. It meant God was happy for his people to eat that food. Some things were clean, like goats, fish, chicken. Some were not, like pigs, prawns and eagles.

- What is the reason for these laws?

You are holy
⊙ **Read: *Deuteronomy 14:1-2, 21***
Explain that God's people are holy. So they must be different from other nations. We do not know why God chose some animals and not others. God has the right to choose. At that time God's chosen people must only eat God's chosen food. This showed that the people of Israel were different.

Do not be like people of other religions
⊙ **Read: *Deuteronomy 14:1, 21***

Some pagans cut themselves when someone died. Some pagans cooked a young goat in its mother's milk as magic. The people of Israel must be different. They must eat and live differently from pagans.

① **Apply:** Christians can eat every food. Jesus said all foods are clean (Mark 7:19). Peter had a vision to show all foods are clean. The gospel of Jesus is for all people. Give thanks to God for the freedom to eat that Jesus gives.

The reason for the law in Deuteronomy 14 is still important. God's people must be different from unbelievers. Paul said to the Corinthians they can eat food offered to idols, but not if that tempts another Christian to eat what they think is sinful. Christians are free to eat and not eat. But we must love and help others.

If you are invited to a religious meal that is not Christian, think carefully. If you eat, will others thinks that you accept another religion?

⬆ **Pray:** *Ask God for wisdom to know when it is best not to eat something. Ask God for love for other Christians so you do not tempt them to sin.*

⬇ STUDY: Deuteronomy 14:22-29

24 DO CHRISTIANS HAVE TO GIVE A TENTH?

❂ Background
Moses is giving the people of Israel the laws for how to live in the promised land. The laws show how to love God and love other people.

⊙ Read verses 22-29.
Read each verse and explain it to yourself in your own words.

❂ Notes
- **Deuteronomy 14:23.** "Tithe" means one tenth.

- **Deuteronomy 14:23.** "Revere" means to honour.

- **Deuteronomy 14:27.** "Allotment or inheritance" (NIV). The tribe of Levi does not own land.

⊙ Something to work on
- *How does giving a tithe teach people to fear God?*

Verse 23. We may try to save our grain and money, try to be rich and try to have enough for bad times. When we do that, we trust in ourselves. Giving a tithe makes God's people have less, but they also learn to put God first and revere him.

Verses 24-26. The place of offering is the place of worship in Deuteronomy 12:5. Many people would live far from the place of offering. To carry all the grain and animals was hard. So the people of Israel could sell their tithe, take the money, and then buy food to offer when they got there.

Verse 27. The tribe of Levi were priests. They had no land, crops or animals. The Levites also joined the offerers and ate with them.

Verses 28-29. Every third year, the tithe was given for the poor. Poor people did not own land. The poor were Levites, aliens, fatherless and widows. The tithe helped to care for the poor.

What does this law say to Christians? The New Testament does not give a tithe law. But the New Testament encourages Christians to be very glad and generous to give for Christian ministry and the poor, to thank God and learn to fear him. This probably means some people give more than a tenth.

- *Do people in your church give tithes? What are their reasons for giving?*

⊕ MAIN POINT
Give generously to God.

➔ TEACH: Deuteronomy 14:22-29

⊙ Start
God loves a cheerful giver.
• Do you give cheerfully?

Give to God
⊙ **Read: *Deuteronomy 14:22-27***
God has given his people everything. They must remember him when their crops grow and animals reproduce. All the people of Israel must give one tenth of everything, every year. They must go to the place for sacrifice that God chooses. The people can eat the offering but they must include the Levite priests, who have no land.

Give to others
⊙ **Read: *Deuteronomy 14:28-29***
In the third year, the tithe is given to the poor: Levites, aliens, fatherless and widows. These people do not own land. They have no crops or animals to give. They need help from others. God wants his people who have much to give to those who have little. Why give?

There are four reasons for giving.
1. God wants his people to thank him for his blessing. The people must rejoice (v26).
2. God wants his people to learn to revere the LORD (v23). *Explain to your listeners how the tithe helps people to trust and fear God.*
3. God wants his people to provide for the priests. The priests serve the people, teach the people the law and organise the sacrifices.
4. God wants his people to care for the poor Israelites.

⊙ **Apply:** Christians disagree about giving a tenth of all they produce and earn. The New Testament does not tell Christians to give one tenth of everything to God. But the New Testament does not stop this law.

The four reasons for the law still stand. 1. Christians must give to thank God. 2. Christians must fear God. 3. Christians must give for Christian ministry. 4. Christians must care for the poor.

All the reasons for the Old Testament law are the same for Christians.

Many Christians can give more than one tenth. Some Christians cannot. The important thing is to have a thankful heart and give as much as we can. This passage shows us how to love God with all our heart, and love our neighbour as ourselves. If we love, we will be generous.

⊙ **Pray:** *Ask God to make us generous, thankful and joyful. Ask God to give us love for him and for the poor. Thank God for his many blessings to us.*

⬇ STUDY: Deuteronomy 15:1-18

25 GIVE GENEROUSLY TO THOSE IN NEED

❂ Background
Moses prepares the Israelites to live in the promised land. He encourages the people to obey the laws from God.

⊙ Read verses 1-18.
Read the passage 2 or 3 times. Read each verse and explain it to yourself in your own words.

❂ Notes
- **Deuteronomy 15:7, 10.**
"Hardhearted", "grudging heart" means unwilling.
- **Deuteronomy 15:7, 11.**
"Tightfisted" (NIV) means selfish. "Openhanded" (NIV) means willing to lend. God's people should be generous.

⊙ Something to work on
These laws protect needy Israelites. The first law (v1-11) cancels debts. The second law is about slaves.

Verses 1-6. If an Israelite borrowed money from you, then you must cancel the debt in the seventh year. The reason is to stop people being poor (v4). If the people of Israel share, then God will bless the people. There will be enough for everyone.

- *Why was this law was hard to keep?*

Verses 7-11. Imagine the seventh year is near. An Israelite wants to borrow money. "But," you think, "he has no time to pay back my money. I will not lend." God's people must not think like this. They must be generous and not greedy.

Verse 4 says: "There should be no poor among you". Verse 11 says: "There will always be poor". Verse 4 is what should happen. But because people are greedy, verse 11 is true.

Verses 12-18. If an Israelite was really poor, he could become a slave. His master must be an Israelite. The master must look after him. After six years, the slave could go free. The master must give him much food.

Christians do not have a fixed year to cancel debts. But the reasons behind the law still stand. We must care for Christians in need. We must share if we have more than we need (Acts 4:32). We must help fellow Christians who have no work.

- *What examples can you give your listeners for your place?*

⊕ MAIN POINT
There should be no needy people among the people of God.

⊙ TEACH: Deuteronomy 15:1-18

⊙ Start
How do we help our brothers and sisters in special need? In ancient Israel, God's people had laws to help the poor.

Be generous to lend to those in need
⊙ **Read:** *Deuteronomy 15:1-11*
Tell your listeners what the law about cancelling debts says. God's people could be poor for many reasons. Maybe they got sick. Maybe they were not good farmers. God promises to give enough to all his people, but they must share.

⊕ **Illustration:** *Use verses 9-10 as an illustration of greedy thinking. This law says God's people must be generous and open their hands to give.*

⊙ **Apply:** How do Christians obey this law today? Christians must care for needy Christians. We must be generous, and give and lend where needed. We must help needy Christians in our place and in other countries. Examples:

- You lend money to a Christian in need. After six years, you cancel the debt.
- A Christian asks you to lend money for his investment project. You say no because he is not poor. This law is not for this situation.
- There are poor Christians in another country. You give money through a church organisation.

Be generous to give work to the poor
⊙ **Read:** *Deuteronomy 15:12-18*
An Israelite may be so poor that he must work for someone else. Maybe he cannot run his own farm, but he can sell himself as a slave. The owner must look after his slave and set him free after six years.

⊙ **Apply:** Christians must find ways to help Christians who are poor and need a job. This is a good and generous thing to do. It may be costly for the employer.
Some examples to think about:

- A church may employ a poor church member to do jobs.
- A Christian businessman may employ a fellow Christian to give him a job.
- Christians can give to Christian organisations that create jobs for poorer Christians in other countries.

God blesses his people but God also expects his people to be generous. We must trust God's blessing. God is generous to us. All we have comes from God.

⊙ **Pray:** *Ask God to help you be generous to give and lend to brothers and sisters in bigger need than you are.*

STUDY: Deuteronomy 16:1-17

26 REMEMBER AND CELEBRATE WHAT GOD HAS DONE

Background
Moses is encouraging the people of Israel to obey God's laws.

Read verses 1-17.

Notes
- **Deuteronomy 16:3.** "Leavened" (NIV). Leaven is the same as yeast. Unleavened bread was quick to cook.
- **Deuteronomy 16:13.** "Tabernacles" (NIV) or "shelters" (GN) are like tents. The people lived in tents during the festival to remember living in tents in the desert.

Something to work on
Israel had festivals (celebrations) each year: **1. Passover** (Exodus 12:1-28; Leviticus 23:4-8), **2. Weeks** (Leviticus 23:15-21), **3. Tabernacles/Shelters** (Leviticus 23:33-44).

- *What must the people remember for each festival? What do they celebrate?*

Verses 1-8. Passover reminded the people of God rescuing them from Egypt. Because the people left Egypt in a hurry, they only used unleavened bread at this festival.

Verses 9-12. The Festival of Weeks was a thanksgiving for the grain harvest. The people were to rejoice in God's blessing. The poor people who did not own land must be included in the festival. The people must remember they were slaves in Egypt.

Verses 13-15. The Festival of Shelters was at the end of the harvest. The poor people without land must be included. The people must celebrate and remember all that God gave them.

Verses 16-17. All three festivals happened at the place God chose.
- *What do these festivals say to Christians?*

1. Jesus is our Passover lamb (1 Corinthians 5:7). Christians celebrate Jesus' death for us at the Lord's Supper or Communion.
2. Weeks is called Pentecost in Greek. Christians celebrate God giving his Holy Spirit to write his law on our hearts.
3. Shelters is in John 7:37-39. Jesus gives streams of living water, which is the Holy Spirit. Christians celebrate Jesus and the gift of the Spirit.

⊕ MAIN POINT
God's people must remember what God has done for them, and celebrate.

➔ TEACH: Deuteronomy 16:1-17

⊙ Start:
For God's people, festivals are important to remember and rejoice in God. God's people in the Old Testament had important festivals.

Festival of Passover
⊙ **Read: *Deuteronomy 16:1-8***
Tell your listeners the background to the Passover and the people's rescue from Egypt. The important points are:
- **Remember** what God did (v1, 3, 6).
- **Rejoice** (v1).

What does this festival say to Christians? Jesus is our Passover lamb. His death rescues us from slavery to sin. This is more important than the rescue of the people of Israel from Egypt. We must remember and rejoice always.

Festival of Weeks
⊙ **Read: *Deuteronomy 16:9-12***
Tell your listeners the background to this festival. The important points are:
- **Remember.** The people must remember they were slaves in Egypt (v12).
- **Rejoice** (v10, 11).
- **Include** all the people (v11).

What does this festival say to Christians? In the New Testament this festival is called **Pentecost**. Pentecost is when God gave his Holy Spirit to all his people. The Holy Spirit writes God's law on our hearts. We give thanks for God's Spirit and walk in the Spirit.

Festival of Shelters
⊙ **Read: *Deuteronomy 16:13-15***
Tell your listeners the background to this festival. The important points are:
- **Remember**. The people remembered living in tents in the desert. God gave all they needed in that time.
- **Rejoice** (v14, 15).
- **Include** all the people (v14).

What does this festival say to Christians? When Jesus celebrated the Festival of Shelters in John 7, he promised the Holy Spirit as a stream of living water (John 7:37-39). God gave water in the desert. Jesus gives the living water of his Spirit.

⊙ **Apply:** Christians must remember and celebrate what God has done for them in Jesus. The Lord's Supper or Communion is our main festival to remember Jesus' death. We must celebrate this regularly with praise and thanks in our hearts to Jesus. The people of Israel had to make a long journey for the festivals. Christians can celebrate anywhere.

⊙ **Pray:** *Give God thanks for Jesus and his death on the cross, which rescues us from sin. Thank God for the wonderful gift of his Holy Spirit, who lives in all believers.*

⬇ STUDY: Deuteronomy 17:14-20

27 UNDER GOD'S RULE

❈ Background
Moses is preparing the people of Israel to have a king. He tells them what sort of a king they must have.

⊙ Read verses 14-20.
Read the passage 2 or 3 times.

❈ Notes
Deuteronomy 17:16. "Many horses" (NIV) means a strong army. "Return to Egypt" (NIV) means to rely on another country.

Deuteronomy 17:17. "Accumulate" (NIV) means to get a lot.

Deuteronomy 17:18. "A copy of this law" (NIV) means the book of Deuteronomy.

⊙ Something to work on
Later, the people of Israel will ask for a king (1 Samuel 8). Before then, Joshua, and judges like Gideon and Samson, led the people.

Notice the things the king must be like:
- A man God chooses (v15)
- An Israelite, not a foreigner (v15)
- Not trust in an army or strength (v16)
- Not have many wives to lead his heart away from God (v17)
- Not have too much money (v17)
- Write and read God's law (v18-19)
- Revere, honour and obey God (v19)
- Not be proud (v20)

A strong army, many wives and much money are temptations. They can lead a king away from God. That is why the king must write his own copy of God's law. The king must read God's law to know it and obey it. This means the king is under God's rule. All the people of God must read God's word (Psalm 1:2). The king is no different from the people.

Most kings did not obey this law. In 1 and 2 Kings, almost every king is bad. Solomon (1 Kings 2 – 11) did all the bad things in this law. He had horses, many wives and much money. His heart went away from God.

God is the true King. God ruled Israel's kings through his law. The law about the king helps us look to Jesus, the perfect King. Jesus is King of the church. This law is not about kings and rulers of nations today.

⊕ MAIN POINT
The leader of God's people must be under God. Only Jesus did this perfectly.

➔ TEACH: Deuteronomy 17:14-20

➔ Start
Many countries have kings. Kings are often powerful rulers.
- What is the ideal or best king like?

The people of Israel had many bad kings. None of them were perfect.

Three warnings about a king
➔ **Read:** *Deuteronomy 17:16-17*
Kings must not have many horses. Many horses make a king trust in his own strength and not in God.

Kings must not have many wives. Many wives may tempt a king away from God.

Kings must not have lots of money. Money is a temptation away from God.

Tell your listeners how King Solomon failed in all three of these things.

A king under God
➔ **Read:** *Deuteronomy 17:14-15, 18-20*
The king must be under God. He must not do what he thinks or wants. God chooses the king. The king must be an Israelite. He must write a copy of the law and read the law all his days. The king must honour God. The king must not be proud.

Christians are not a nation like the people of ancient Israel. We do not have a king over us as they did. God's people today are the church. This law tells us about leaders for the church. Church leaders must be under God's rule. Church leaders must be true believers. Church leaders must be humble and know God's word.

Some church leaders are not under God's rule. Some do not know God's word very well. Some are proud. Some church leaders want power and money. Some church leaders do sexual sin. These are not good things. God is not happy with leaders like this.

The perfect King
Explain to your listeners that the people of Israel never had a perfect king. Jesus, Son of David, was the perfect King. He was always under God's law. Jesus was not tempted by many horses, power, wives or money. Jesus is King of the church. Christians belong to his kingdom. Christians are to live under his rule.

⚡ **Apply:** What temptations do the leaders of the church have in your place? *Encourage church leaders to live under God's word. Urge church members to pray for church leaders.*

🙏 **Pray:** *Thank God for Jesus, the perfect King. Pray for the leaders of the church. Pray they will live under God's rule.*

STUDY: Deuteronomy 18:9-19

28 LISTEN TO GOD'S PROPHETS

Background
Moses will soon die. After he dies, God will still speak to the people by prophets.

Read verses 9-19.
Read the passage 2 or 3 times.

Notes
Deuteronomy 18:9. "Detestable" (NIV), "disgusting" (GN) means God hates these things.

Deuteronomy 18:10. "Divination" is asking the spirits or magic man to show the future or to show who was responsible for what was done. "Omens" are signs from bad people or spirits about what will happen.

Deuteronomy 18:11. A "medium or spiritist" (NIV) is a person who says they can talk to dead people. "Cast/use spells" is to use magic on someone.

Something to work on
Verses 9-14. Some people who worshipped other gods sacrificed children as an offering to the gods. That was a very bad thing to do. Other religions had people who said they could tell the future. Like a witch or magic man, they may use magic on people. They may try to speak to the dead to find out the future or use a shaman or spirit medium.

- *What things like this are done in your place?*

All these things mislead people. They come from Satan, who lies. These things are detestable and disgusting to God. God's people must not go to the magic man or witch or other people like that.

God is in control of everything. God tells his people everything they need to know. That is why the bad things in verses 9-14 are followed by what is right in verses 15-18.

Verses 15-18. God will send a prophet like Moses for his people. The prophet will speak God's words to the people.

In the Old Testament we see many prophets like Moses: Elijah, Elisha, Amos, and more. But the main prophet like Moses is Jesus. When Jesus was baptised, God's voice from heaven said: "Listen to him!" For Christians today, God still speaks to us by his word, the Bible, written and explained.

⊕ MAIN POINT
God speaks by his prophets — listen to them! Do not follow magic or sorcery.

➜ TEACH: Deuteronomy 18:9-19

⊙ Start
People like to know the future. But people often go to the wrong people to find out the future. *Give some examples from your place.*

Wrong ways to look for what God says
⊙ **Read:** *Deuteronomy 18:9-14*
Moses tells the people not to go to people who say they can speak to dead people or get messages from them. Some of those people use magic on people. Some of those people look for signs for the future. Some unbelievers even kill their children as an offering to their gods. All these things are very bad. Horoscopes, magic, witchdoctors and shamans are all wrong. God hates these things.

Explain to your listeners that these things are tricks from Satan. Do not be tricked! Stars and magic do not rule us. Only God rules. Even if Christians do these bad things, do not follow them. Keep away from Satan, who tricks and tells lies. But God controls life and death. Death without God is what Satan wants. But death without God is hell.

Do not be scared of the wrong things. What if a witch or magic man uses magic on you? Remember God is more powerful. Nothing can keep us away from the love of God in Jesus.

Right ways to hear what God says
⊙ **Read:** *Deuteronomy 18:15-19*
If we want to know what God says, it is easy! After Moses dies, God will raise up other prophets like Moses. Those prophets will speak God's word to the people. *Tell your listeners about some of the prophets in the Old Testament.* God warns the people that they must listen to true prophets.

The greatest prophet and believers today
The greatest prophet is Jesus. When he was baptised, God's voice from heaven said: **"Listen to him!"**

Believers today must listen to what God says. God speaks in the Bible. There God has spoken by his prophets and by his Son, Jesus (Hebrews 1:1-4). We must listen and obey.

God speaks clearly. His word is not difficult. We must not follow the ways of other gods to find out the future. We must listen to and obey God's word, the Bible.

⇧ **Pray:** *Thank God that he speaks clearly in his word. Pray you will listen to his word more and obey it.*

STUDY: Deuteronomy 22:1-12

29 — EVERYTHING IN LIFE IS TO BE DONE FOR GOD

Background
Moses is preparing the people for living in the promised land. He gives them the laws from God. The laws are about all parts of life.

Read verses 1-12.
Read the passage 2 or 3 times. Read each verse and explain it to yourself in your own words.

Notes
Deuteronomy 22:8. "Parapet" (NIV) is a fence around a flat roof to stop people falling off.

Deuteronomy 22:12. "Tassel" is some extra cloth at the end of a coat, cloth or scarf that hangs down like a frill or fringe.

Something to work on
Some of these laws are strange. Try to work out what is the reason for each law before you read on.

Verses 1-4. God's people must look after the animals of other Israelites. This is one way of loving our neighbour. Christians also must care for other Christians. What if your brother's goat wanders off? You must look after it and return it.

Verse 5. This law is about people trying to be different from how God made them. It does not mean a woman cannot wear jeans or a man cannot wear a sarong.

Verses 6-7. This law is to make sure there can be more food in the future. We must look after our food supply and resources.

Verse 8. In ancient Israel, people had flat roofs and sometimes worked or slept on the roof. A parapet protects people from falling off. God's people must make sure their buildings are safe for others.
- *How can people make their houses safe in your place? Are cooking areas safe for children? Is electricity safe?*

Verses 9-11. Mixing seeds, animals and cloth was probably something people of other religions did. God's people must not do things that people of other religions do.

Verse 12. Tassels reminded God's people to keep the law. Read Numbers 15:38-39. God's people today do not need tassels. God's Spirit has written the law in our hearts if we are true believers. But we do need to remember God's law.

⊕ MAIN POINT
Do everything for God.

➡ TEACH: Deuteronomy 22:1-12

⊙ Start
Do these laws seem strange? When we know the reason for the law, we can think about what it says today.

Look after other Christians' lost things
⊙ **Read: *Deuteronomy 22:1-4***
Tell your listeners the reason for this law. It is easy for Christians today to ignore problems of other people. But we belong together as God's people. We must care for each other. *Give an example for your place.*

Be who God made you to be
⊙ **Read: *Deuteronomy 22:5***
In some countries, people have operations to change from being a man or woman. Christians must not do that. We must accept who we are. God made us.

Think of future need for food
⊙ **Read: *Deuteronomy 22:6-7***
We must also make sure there will be food for our children and children's children. We must look after the world's resources in our land.

Make sure our homes are safe
⊙ **Read: *Deuteronomy 22:8***
Tell your listeners why the people of Israel needed this law.

- Is your home safe? Is your church building safe? *Give some examples of making your place safe.* Think of old people or children. Can they hurt themselves in your home? Are the stairs safe for people to use? What do you need to do to make your home safer?

Do not follow the ways of other religions
⊙ **Read: *Deuteronomy 22:9-11***
Probably unbelievers mixed things like animals, seeds and materials. Maybe there was magic. God's people must not do the things of wrong religion.

Remember the laws
⊙ **Read: *Deuteronomy 22:12***
Tell your listeners why the people of Israel had tassels. Explain to them the difference for Christians. Challenge your listeners to make sure they remember God's law.

Every part of our life must be lived for God—our home life, clothing, food and neighbour's animals. We must always think of what God wants us to do. God is God of all of our lives. Everything must be done for him.

⬆ **Pray:** *Ask God for understanding about how to obey his laws today. Give thanks that we are forgiven in Jesus when we fail.*

STUDY: Deuteronomy 22:13-30

30 YOU MUST NOT DO SEXUAL SIN

Background
Moses prepares the people of God to live in the promised land. He gives them the laws from God and encourages the people to obey them.

Read verses 13-30.
Read the passage 2 or 3 times.

Notes
Deuteronomy 22:14. "Proof of her virginity" (NIV) means to show that the woman never had sex before she married. The evidence is a bedsheet with her blood on it.

Deuteronomy 22:21. "Promiscuous" (NIV) means to have sex with more than one person.

Deuteronomy 22:22. "Sleeping with" (NIV), "intercourse" (GN) means to have sex with someone.

Deuteronomy 22:23. "Pledged" (NIV) means engaged.

Deuteronomy 22:25. "Rape" means for a man to force himself on a woman for sex.

Something to work on
Sex is not an easy subject to talk about. Some people feel shame. Some think it is funny. The Bible speaks about sex many times. Sex is a big temptation for many people. Believers need to be encouraged to be pure.

Verses 13-22. A man may make up a story that his wife already had sex before they married. This may be an excuse to end the marriage. The parents maybe can prove the man is telling lies. Marriage is important and divorce must not be easy.

Verses 23-27. If a man rapes an engaged woman, the woman will cry for help. In the city, people will hear her cry. In the country they may not. Men must not force themselves on women. That is bad.

Verses 28-30. What if a man and woman have sex but the woman is not engaged? They must marry, even if the man rapes or forces himself on her. This is because it will be hard for the woman to get a husband. The man must care for her.

Christian marriage is meant to be like the relationship between Christ and the church (Ephesians 5:22-33).

MAIN POINT
Be faithful to your wife or husband. No sex outside marriage.

➔ TEACH: Deuteronomy 22:13-30

⌄ Start
People in our world love sex. There is much wrong sexual behaviour everywhere. Christians must not be silent on this important topic. God has plenty to say about it and so must we.

Sex is a wonderful gift from God for marriage. It is for a husband and wife to enjoy. But sex is wrong outside marriage.

In ancient Israel, bad sinners were put to death. For Christians, bad sinners cannot stay in the church. They are removed from church membership.

Be faithful and pure in marriage
⌄ **Read:** *Deuteronomy 22:13-22*
Tell your listeners what these verses are about. God's people must treat marriage as special. Christian husbands and wives must do everything they can to make their marriage strong and loving.

Do not force yourself on a woman
⌄ **Read:** *Deuteronomy 23:23-27*
What if an engaged woman had sex with a man? If they both agreed, they were put to death. What if the man forced the woman? The man was put to death if he forced the woman.

Many men do not control their desire for sex. They force women to have sex. God is not happy with this. Women must be treated with honour.

If a man forces a woman for sex, we must report to the police.

Another case
⌄ **Read:** *Deuteronomy 23:28-29*
If a man forced himself on a woman who was not engaged, what happened? In this case, they must marry. This law protected the woman. It forced the man to care for her. If the woman did not want to marry him, probably she did not have to marry him. Today, if a man forces a woman, Christians should care for the woman. She must not be made to feel shame.

There are many more laws about sex in the Bible. Wrong sex is a powerful temptation. God's people must be pure. Marriage must be honoured.

Husbands and wives must love each other as God loves his people. In Ephesians 5:22-33, Paul gives the example of Jesus and the church for husbands and wives to follow.

⬆ **Pray:** *Ask God to make you pure in sex. Thank God that Jesus forgives past sins.*

STUDY: Deuteronomy 26:1-11

31 GIVE THANKS FOR WHAT GOD HAS DONE

Background
This section is the end of the laws. Moses finishes telling the people all the laws from God.

Read verses 1-11.
Read the passage 2 or 3 times. Read each verse and explain it to yourself in your own words.

Notes
Deuteronomy 26:5. "Aramean." Jacob's forefathers came from outside the promised land, from Haran and Aram.

Deuteronomy 26:9. "Milk and honey" (NIV) means good, sweet food and drink.

Something to work on
This was the last law Moses gave the people. It was about a special offering of thanks when the people arrived in the land. It was a law to obey only one time.

Verses 1-4. God promised the land to Abraham a long time before Moses. God keeps his promise. The land is a good land. It will produce many crops and animals.

When the people of Israel settle in the land, they must offer to God the first things from the land.

Verses 5-9. These verses tell the story of God's people. Jacob went to Egypt, where his son Joseph was (Genesis 46). Jacob died there and his family grew to be a large nation at the beginning of the book of Exodus. Then Pharaoh, the king of Egypt, made the people of Israel to be slaves (Exodus 1). The people cried out to God (Exodus 2:23-25). God answered their cry. God sent Moses to lead the people out of Egypt. "Mighty hand" (NIV, v8) and "great terror" mean the punishments God brought against Pharaoh (Exodus 7 – 12).

It is important for God's people to remember what God has done.

- *For Christians, what do we have to remember and celebrate? How good are we at doing that?*

Verses 10-11. Because God was faithful, the people in thanks give back to God the first things from the ground. God gives food. Other gods do not do that. The people must rejoice. How good are we at rejoicing in what God gives us? Read Philippians 4:4.

⊕ MAIN POINT
God's people must give thanks to God.

➔ TEACH: Deuteronomy 26:1-11

⌄ Start
- Do you sometimes forget God when things are good?
  This law helps the people of God remember to give thanks to God.

Offer God the first and best
⌄ Read: *Deuteronomy 26:1-4*

When the people settle in the land, God asks for the first of the crops and fruit from the land. This means giving to God comes first.

- How do we put God first and give thanks to him?

Remember what God has done
⌄ Read: *Deuteronomy 26:5-9*

These words are the story of God's people. *Tell your listeners the story of Jacob, Egypt, the nation, slavery, rescue and into the promised land.*

God's people need to remember what God did. That is why reading the Bible story is important. What is our story? For Christians, the centre of our story is Jesus on the cross. That is our rescue. Jesus rescues sinners from slavery to sin. He brings people from spiritual death to spiritual life.

- What songs does your church sing that tell the story of Jesus' death and resurrection?

Worship and rejoice
⌄ Read: *Deuteronomy 26:10-11*

The passage ends with the command to bow down and rejoice. Joy is very important for God's people. The New Testament also commands Christians to rejoice. When we think what God did for us, we will have joy in our hearts. When we remember what God gives us, we will be thankful from our hearts.

A good example is Ephesians 1:3-14. Paul reminds the Ephesians of what God did for them. As he tells them, he is thankful and joyful and praises God.

- How joyful are you?
- How thankful are you to God?

Encourage your listeners to write down all the things God did for them. Encourage your listeners to tell others what God did for them. Encourage your listeners to praise and worship God with joy.

God chose his people. God rescued his people. God brought his people into a good land. For Christians, God chose us. God rescued us in Jesus. God is bringing us to a perfect heavenly land. Rejoice! *Sing some songs that tell what Jesus did for us. Praise and worship him.*

⌅ **Pray:** *Thank God for everything he did for you. Rejoice in the Lord!*

STUDY: Deuteronomy 27:1-13

32 STAY RIGHT WITH GOD

Background
Moses tells the people to have a ceremony after they enter the promised land. This is a ceremony for one time only, in a special place.

Read verses 1-13.
Read the passage 2 or 3 times. Read each verse and explain it to yourself in your own words.

Notes
Deuteronomy 27:3. "Words of this law" means Deuteronomy 1 – 26.

Deuteronomy 27:12. "Pronounce" means to tell out.

Something to work on
There are four things that the people of Israel must do:

1. They must write the words of Deuteronomy 1 – 26 on large stones. The stones are covered in plaster, probably to make the writing clear (v2-3, 8).

2. They must make an altar of stones. The stones must not be cut with an iron tool (v5-6).

3. They must offer a burnt offering (v6). The rules of burnt offerings are in Leviticus 1. It is a sacrifice for sin.

4. They then offer a fellowship offering. The rules of fellowship offerings are in Leviticus 3. It is a sacrifice that enjoys fellowship with God. Some of the animal is kept for people to eat (v7).

- *What does this ceremony mean?*

The stones and altar are put on Mount Ebal. In verse 13, Mount Ebal is the mountain of curse.

- *Why are the stones and altar not on Mount Gerizim, the mountain of blessing?*

This ceremony means the law from God leads to a curse if it is not obeyed. The people will fail to keep the law. They will be under God's curse. Read Deuteronomy 27:26. But God gives a way out from the curse: burnt offerings for sin. Then the people can enjoy fellowship with God in the fellowship offering.

- *How do we see the burnt offering and fellowship offering fulfilled in the New Testament?*

Read Galatians 3:10-14.
How can people today be free from the curse of breaking God's law?

⊕ MAIN POINT
God gives a way for sinful people to be right with him.

⮕ TEACH: Deuteronomy 27:1-13

⊙ Start

Give an example of a special ceremony from your place. God gave the people of Israel rules for a special ceremony. This ceremony would happen after the Israelites entered the promised land. The ceremony only happened one time.

Four things the people must do
⊙ Read: *Deuteronomy 27:2-7*

Tell your listeners the four things the people of Israel must do:
1. Write the law on stones covered in plaster.
2. Make an altar.
3. Offer a burnt offering for sin.
4. Offer a fellowship sacrifice.

Explain to your listeners the meaning of this ceremony. The ceremony is on Mount Ebal. That is the mountain of curse (v13). No person can keep all God's law. People sin and are under a curse because of their disobedience to God (v26).

But God gives a way out from the curse. God gives laws for a burnt offering for forgiveness from sin. Then the people can celebrate fellowship with God.

Jesus fulfils the ceremony

For us today, Jesus fulfils the law and sacrifices. We must not offer animal sacrifices. Jesus is our sacrifice for sin. Believers are not under a curse for their sin. Jesus takes away our curse. We enjoy fellowship with God because of Jesus.

Read Galatians 3:10-14 and explain these verses carefully to your listeners. Show them that God forgives our sin when we have faith in Jesus alone.

The law of the Old Testament leads us to Jesus. Only Jesus kept the law perfectly. We do not. When we sin and fail to keep the law, we must turn to Jesus for forgiveness.

⚠ Apply:
For your listeners who are believers, this message is full of joy. In verse 7, the people of Israel must rejoice. Christians have much more reason to rejoice. Jesus is so much better than animal sacrifices.

For your listeners who are not believers, invite them to trust in Jesus. Jesus takes away the curse of sin on the cross. So anyone who trusts Jesus is free from the curse which comes from disobedience. They can enjoy fellowship with God.

⮝ Pray:
Give thanks to God for giving us a way to escape from the curse for sin. Thank God for Jesus. Pray for unbelievers to put their trust in Jesus for forgiveness and fellowship with God.

STUDY: Deuteronomy 28:1-14

33 BE BLESSED BY GOD!

Background
Moses is encouraging the people of Israel to obey all the laws God gave them. In this section, he tells them the blessings that the people will get if they obey God.

Read verses 1-14.
Read the passage 2 or 3 times.

Notes
Deuteronomy 28:3. "In the city" and "in the country" (NIV). Country is rural areas. City and country means everywhere, in every place.
Deuteronomy 28:6. "When you come in" and "when you go out" (NIV) mean at every time.
Deuteronomy 28:7. "Flee from you in seven" (NIV) means the enemy will lose and run in every direction.
Deuteronomy 28:13. "The head, not the tail" (NIV) means the people of Israel will be the leading nation.

Something to work on
Think about two groups of blessings.

1. List the verses and blessings that are about producing more things. This includes rain, food, crops, animals, children and many things.
- *What do you think the people of Israel will be like if they are blessed by God?*

Unbelievers in the land thought other gods gave rain and children. But it is the true God who gives rain and children.

2. List the verses and blessings that are about other nations and God protecting his people.
- *In what ways will blessed Israelites be different from the other nations?*

Find the verses that tell the people what they must do to get blessing from God. The people must fully obey.
- *Are these blessings the same for Christians today?*

Christians belong to the kingdom of God. We are not a nation on earth. Christian blessings are mainly spiritual (Ephesians 1:3). The blessings of the Sermon on the Mount (Matthew 5:1-12) are about the kingdom of heaven. Many Christians get this wrong. They think God wants them to be rich on earth. Our treasure is in heaven.

Because Jesus died for us, we can be sure we have spiritual blessing in him already. Christians are righteous in Jesus through faith. But our faith must also show obedience in our lives.

MAIN POINT
God wants to bless his people.

⊙ TEACH: Deuteronomy 28:1-14

⊙ Start
- Are you blessed by God? What blessings does God give you?

Blessed with many things
⊙ **Read:** *Deuteronomy 28:3-6, 8, 11, 12*
God promised the people of Israel that they will be blessed with many things: rain, children, crops, food, animals (v3-6, 8, 11, 12). They will be rich.

Blessed as a strong nation
⊙ **Read:** *Deuteronomy 28:7, 10, 13*
God also promised Israel that their nation will be strong. Enemies will not defeat them. Other nations will not rule over them (v7, 10, 13).

God wanted his people to be a strong and blessed nation so that other nations will be blessed by God.

How to be blessed
⊙ **Read:** *Deuteronomy 1-2, 9,13-14*
Moses gave the people God's laws in chapters 5-26. Now he encourages them to obey everything God commanded them. God wants full obedience.

- Are these blessings still the same for Christians?

⊕ **Illustration:** A preacher tells his listeners that God wants Christians to be wealthy. He says being rich is God's blessing and it is good to have expensive cars, much land, houses, gold and things. Some Christians who hear this become sad because they are poor. They think God has not blessed them. Some rich Christians think they must be very good people because they are rich. Is this right?

⊙ **Apply:** Jesus preached about the kingdom of heaven. God's people are not a nation on earth now. Jesus taught some blessings in Matthew 5:1-12. *Tell your listeners what the blessings are in these verses. Read Ephesians 1:3-14.* The blessings in these verses are spiritual. They are wonderful things like forgiveness, being a child of God and having God's Holy Spirit.

We have many physical blessings from God. But because of Jesus, the most important blessings are spiritual or heavenly. We should want these things first.

These spiritual blessings are ours in Jesus through faith (Ephesians 1:3). Our faith must show obedience to God. We do not rely on our obedience but we rely on Jesus.

⊙ **Pray:** *Thank God for the spiritual blessings through Jesus. Thank God for choosing you, forgiving you, making you his child, and giving you his Holy Spirit.*

⬇ STUDY: Deuteronomy 28:15-68

34 DO NOT DISOBEY GOD

❂ Background
Moses gave the people God's law in Deuteronomy 5 – 26. Then Moses encouraged them to obey with the blessings in Deuteronomy 28:1-14. Now Moses warns the people what God will do if they disobey his law.

⊙ Read verses 15-44.
Read the passage 2 or 3 times.

⊛ Notes
- **Deuteronomy 28:15.** "Curses" (NIV) are the opposite of blessing. They are not magic. Curses are God's punishment for sin.

- **Deuteronomy 28:23.** "Sky over your head will be bronze" (NIV) means there will be no rain.

⊙ Something to work on
Think how God is in control of everything. See which verses show God is in control of: weather, life and death, crops and animals, sickness and other nations
- Which curses are the opposites of the blessings in verses 1-14?
- What will it be like for someone under God's curse in verses 30-34?
- How will you feel?

⊙ Read verses 45-68.
- *How are the things in these verses more difficult than in verses 15-44?*

For ancient Israel, if they disobey God, God will curse the people. This passage is about the people together. It is not about cursing one person. If the people together disobey, the whole nation of Israel will suffer.

The biggest sin is worshipping wrong gods. If God's people want to worship useless idols, God will send the people to another land to worship useless gods of wood or stone (v36).

To be sent from the land is the last curse. The other curses come first. When the first curses happen, God's people can turn back to God. For example, read **Amos 4:6-12**.

Christians have good news. Everyone disobeys God. But Jesus took the curse for us. Read Galatians 3:13-14. By trusting Jesus' death, believers are free from the curse for disobeying the law. We must live with no fear. God is in control of all things.

⊕ MAIN POINT
Do not disobey God. He will punish disobedience.

→ TEACH: Deuteronomy 28:15-68

⊕ Illustration: In Genesis 4, God warned Cain not to sin. But Cain did not listen. Cain killed his brother Abel. God cursed Cain and sent him away from his land.

God warned the people of Israel not to sin. If the Israelites disobey God, God will curse them. He will send them out of the promised land.

What are the curses?
⊙ **Read:** *Deuteronomy 28:15, 20-21, 24-25, 28-29, 36.*
Tell your listeners what things will happen if the people of Israel disobey.

Why will God curse his people?
⊙ **Read:** *Deuteronomy 28:45*
God will punish the people of Israel if they disobey him. The Israelites know God's laws. They must obey God's law or they will get God's curse.

Only God can curse
Tell your listeners that God is in control of everything. God controls the weather, sickness, life and death, crops and animals, and other nations. Only God is in control. The curses are not magic. No one else has the power to curse.

Did Israel listen to this to this warning?
Later in the Old Testament, the curses came on the people of Israel because they disobeyed God. Explain to your listeners the example from Amos 4. The curses were also God's kind way of warning his people to turn back to him. But sadly the people of Israel did not listen to God's warnings. They did not turn back to God. So God took them away from the promised land, as slaves to Babylon.

Are Christians cursed?
The good news is that Jesus takes the curse for sin on the cross. Believers in Jesus are not under a curse. Believers in Jesus are free from the curse. Every person sins. Every person was under a curse because of their disobedience. Jesus died to take the curse so we can be blessed by God.

① **Apply:** *Some listeners may not be believers. Encourage them to trust in Jesus. Some may be afraid of being cursed. Encourage them that no other person can curse a believer in Jesus. Some listeners may think it is ok to disobey God because God will forgive. Warn them not to disobey God. True believers always want to please God.*

↑ **Pray:** *Give thanks that Jesus died to take our curse for our disobedience. Ask God to help us trust in Jesus and live in freedom from fear.*

STUDY: Deuteronomy 30:1-10

35 GOD WILL CHANGE HEARTS

Background
Moses knows the people will disobey. But God promises he will change the hearts of the people so they can obey him.

Read verses 1-10.
Read the passage 2 or 3 times.

Notes
Deuteronomy 30:2. "Return / turn back to God" means to repent, to turn away from sin.
Deuteronomy 30:6. "Circumcise" (NIV) usually means to cut the foreskin. In this verse it is to circumcise the heart. It means God changes your heart to be right with him.

Something to work on
Read Deuteronomy 29:18-28. God knows the hearts of his people will turn away from him (v18). The people will turn away from God (v25-28). They will have to go out of the promised land.

Good news! God will rescue his people and bring them back to the promised land. God will bring his word into the people's hearts (v1 and 6). The people of Israel will then turn to God and obey him and love him (v2, 6, 8, 10).

God will bring the people of Israel back to the promised land and bless them (v3-5, 9). God will keep the promises to Abraham from Genesis 12:2-3.

Read Genesis 17:10-14. God told Abraham to be circumcised. Physical circumcision showed the special relationship with God. But the real problem was not with the body but the heart. The true circumcision is of the heart. God told the people of Israel to circumcise their hearts in Deuteronomy 10:16. Read Romans 2:28-29.

This means God wants his people to love him with all the heart. But God's people have hearts that are stubborn and turn away. People need God to change their hearts. With a changed heart, they will love and obey God (v6-8).

• *When does God change hearts?*

Read Colossians 2:10-11. God changes his people's hearts when they trust in Jesus.

MAIN POINT
God will change hearts so his people can obey him.

➲ TEACH: Deuteronomy 30:1-10

✣ Illustration: A man wanted to obey God fully. Every day he decided he would do everything right for God. But one day he was angry with another person. Another day he was greedy for more money. Another day he wanted the things that belonged to his neighbour.

Why do people not obey God fully? God's law is clear. The problem lies inside us. Our hearts are not right. People need new hearts.

The people of God will fail to obey God in the promised land. God's curses (chapter 28:15-68) will come on the Israelites. They will be taken away from the land.

But that is not the end! There is good news!

What God will do
⊙ **Read:** *Deuteronomy 30:1, 6*
Tell your listeners about physical circumcision from Genesis 17:10-14. Tell them it was a sign of the covenant relationship with God. The true circumcision is of the heart. Read Romans 2: 28, 29 and explain.

What the Israelites will do
⊙ **Read:** *Deuteronomy 30:2,6,8,10*
When God changes the Israelites' hearts, the people will return to God and obey him. People will repent of their sin. People will come back to God. People will love God (v6).

What God will then do
⊙ **Read:** *Deuteronomy 30:3-5, 9*
When the people turn back to God, God will bless them. He will bring them back to the land. God will give them many good things again. They will become many people again. God will keep his promises to Abraham.

When does this happen?
This is good news, but when does it happen? God changes people's hearts when they trust in Jesus. *Read and explain to your listeners Colossians 2:10-11.* When a person trusts Jesus, the Holy Spirit comes into their hearts and changes their hearts.

⚠ **Apply:** *Some listeners may not be believers in Jesus. Encourage them to turn from their sin. Encourage them to turn to Jesus and ask for God's Spirit. If they trust Jesus and turn from sin, then God's Spirit is in their hearts. Encourage them to rely on God's work in their hearts.*

⇧ **Pray:** *Thank God for his wonderful grace to change our hearts so we can love God. Ask God to keep changing us and make us more like Jesus every day.*

STUDY: Deuteronomy 30:11-20

36 CHOOSE LIFE!

◎ Background
Moses is preparing the people for living in the promised land. His sermon ends in these verses.

⊙ Read verses 11-20.
Read the passage 2 or 3 times. Read each verse and explain it to yourself in your own words.

⊗ Notes
Deuteronomy 30:19. "Heaven and earth as witnesses / to witness." God made promises to his people. He wants them to make an agreement to obey him.

⊙ Something to work on
Verses 11-14. Moses encourages the people of Israel to obey God's law. He says it is not too hard to do because God will put it in their hearts so they can do it. Remember what we read in the last section. The problem is the human heart. But God will circumcise or change the heart so his people can obey the law.

- *Where are these verses quoted in the New Testament?*

Read Romans 10:5-9. The word is the good news about Jesus. Paul says that Jesus puts God's word in our hearts and mouths. Moses points to the future. It is the good news of Jesus that puts God's word into our hearts and helps us please God. The gospel is not hard. It is not far away because Jesus brings the gospel to us.

Verses 15-20. This is the last part of the sermon of Moses. Moses challenges the people of Israel to turn to God. He wants the people to choose life, prosperity and blessing. Verse 20 says: "the Lord is your life". Life comes from God, not from the law. God gives life when he changes the hearts of his people (v6).

- *For Christians today, how is God our life?*

Jesus is our life. Jesus is the way, the truth and the life. Life comes from Jesus, who rose from the dead. Jesus changes our hearts so we can love him and live fully for ever. We must choose Jesus.

⊕ MAIN POINT
God wants his people to choose to follow him — and live.

➡ TEACH: Deuteronomy 30:11-20

⊙ Start
The last words people say are often remembered.

- Can you remember any last words someone said to you? Can you remember the last words of a sermon?

Moses ends his sermon with a strong challenge. Choose life!

The word is near you
⊙ Read: *Deuteronomy 30:11-14*
Remember Deuteronomy 30:1-10. God will change the hearts of his people. Moses tells the people of Israel the word of God is not hard to do and not far away. It is in their mouth and heart.

What is Moses speaking about? Paul uses this passage in Romans 10:5-9. The word is the good news of Jesus. The good news is faith in Jesus. This makes us right with God. We cannot be right with God through the law because our hearts are not right.

Choose life!
⊙ Read: *Deuteronomy 30:15-20*
Moses ends the sermon by telling the people to choose life. The people can choose death and destruction and curse. This means the people will disobey God and turn away to other gods. Or they can choose to trust God and follow God. God gives life. This means the people will obey God.

For us, to choose life is to choose Jesus. Jesus is our life. He is the way, truth and life. He gives his life-giving Spirit. Jesus is the resurrection and life. To choose life is to choose God's grace and accept the good news of Jesus.

What a great choice the people can make: life, prosperity, blessing, to live and increase, to live long in the land and to love God. This list excites the people to say yes to God. Tell your listeners what a good thing it is to choose God.

① **Apply:** *Some listeners may not be believers. Encourage them to choose Jesus and live! Encourage them to trust that Jesus' death takes away their sin and curse. Some listeners may be turning away from God. Encourage them to come back to God and choose him again. Encourage them to see the good things that come from choosing Jesus.*

⊕ **Pray:** *Ask God to make our hearts choose him and live. Thank God that Jesus brings the word of the good news near us so we can obey it.*

⬇ STUDY: Deuteronomy 31:1-13

37 FEAR GOD AND DO NOT FEAR THE ENEMY

❈ Background
Moses will soon die. He led the people of Israel for forty years. After his last sermon, Moses hands over to Joshua.

⊖ Read verses 1-13.

❈ Notes
Deuteronomy 31:2. "Not cross the Jordan." Moses is not allowed to enter the land. This is because of Moses' sin in Numbers 20:9-12.
Deuteronomy 31:4. "Sihon and Og." Read Deuteronomy 2:24-3:11.
Deuteronomy 31:10. "Feast of Tabernacles/Shelters." Read Deuteronomy 16:13-15.

⊙ Something to work on
Verses 1-6. Moses speaks to the people of Israel. He tells them he will not enter the land. He tells the people Joshua will lead them. Moses tells the people to obey the laws.
- *What command did Moses give to both the people and to Joshua?*
- *Why did Moses focus on this?*

Forty years before, the people of Israel did not enter the land. They were afraid of the people in the land. Read Deuteronomy 1:27-28. Moses now tells them not to be afraid. He tells them to be strong and full of courage. He reminds the people that God is with them and God will fight for them.

Verses 7-8. Moses speaks to Joshua. Moses also tells Joshua not to be afraid. Joshua must be strong and courageous. God reminds Joshua that God promised land to the descendants of Abraham. God is faithful. Moses reminds Joshua that God is with him.
- *What will make the people and Joshua strong and courageous?*
- *What will make them not fear the enemy?*

Verses 9-13. Every seven years, the priests must read all the law to the people. The people must not forget God's laws. The true leader of God's people is God. God will lead his people by his word and by Joshua. Joshua must be under God and follow God's word.
- *What does this passage say to God's people?*
- *What does it say to leaders?*

⊕ MAIN POINT
Listen to God's word, fear God and do not fear the enemy.

➔ TEACH: Deuteronomy 31:1-13

▸ Start
When leaders of God's people leave or die, people may be afraid of the future. One of the greatest leaders of God's people was Moses. The people knew Moses would die.

Moses encourages the people
◉ **Read: *Deuteronomy 31:1-6***
Moses tells the people to be strong and courageous. The reason the people can be strong and full of courage is because God will lead them. God is powerful and faithful. The enemy is strong. But God is stronger.

Moses encourages Joshua
◉ **Read: *Deuteronomy 31:7-8***
Moses tells Joshua to be strong and courageous. He reminds Joshua that God is faithful to his promise of land. Joshua can be strong and full of courage because God is faithful and powerful.

The people must hear God's word
◉ **Read: *Deuteronomy 31:9-13***
Every seven years the people must hear God's law. The priests must read it to them. The people must learn to fear God. If people fear God, they will not fear an enemy.

When Moses died, Joshua led the people. But the people were also led by God's word. God is the true leader of the people. God leads the people by his word and by his human leader.

✣ Illustration: A church needed to choose a person to be their pastor. One person was popular because he never upset anyone, and always tried to keep everyone happy. The other person was not popular. He was not popular because he did not fear the powerful or rich people who wanted to run the church. Sometimes he would upset the authorities by speaking out God's word.

Who is the better person to be pastor?

① Apply: Who are the best leaders of God's people? The best leaders are under God's word. A leader is strong and courageous only when he or she trusts God and obeys God.

Joshua was not chosen because he had fighting skills, but because he obeyed and trusted God. If you choose a leader for the church, remember what is most important.

God's people all have to be strong and courageous. The leader is not special or different. The way to be strong and full of courage is to trust God's word.

- How often do you read God's word? Do you listen carefully to it and obey it?

⇧ Pray: *Ask God to provide leaders for his church who trust and obey God. Ask God to be the true leader of the church.*

⬇ STUDY: Deuteronomy 32:1-18

38 SING SONGS TO LEARN AND REMEMBER

⊗ Background
Moses wrote a song for the people to sing after he died.

⊙ Read verses 1-18.

⊗ Notes
Deuteronomy 32:2. "Dew" is water on the ground after the cool night.
Deuteronomy 32:5. "Corruptly" (NIV) means badly, wrongly.
Deuteronomy 32:9. "The Lord's portion" (NIV) means the people of Israel are God's special people.
Deuteronomy 32:15. "Jeshurun" (NIV) is a name for the people of Israel. "Sleek" means healthy.

⊙ Something to work on
- *Idea: Can you sing these words to local music?*
- *What do the words of Moses' song teach the people of Israel?*

Verses 1-2. The song begins with a command to listen and learn from God. In the land of Israel, dew was important for water for plants. God's words bring life.

Verses 3-4. *How is God like a rock?*

Verses 5-6. The people of Israel turned away from God. God was their Father but the people did not act like his children.

- *Can you remember examples when the people of Israel turned away from God in the desert?*

See Exodus 32:1-10, Numbers 13:1-33.

- *Can you think when the Israelites turned away from God after Moses died?*

See Joshua 7:1-21, 1 Kings 12:25-33.

Verses 7-14. Write a list of what God did for his people. These things refer to the time in the desert. What does this tell us about God?

Verses 15-18. God looked after the people very well. When God's people are filled with food, they may turn away from God and turn to other gods. This happened in the time of Solomon for example.

Songs must teach us the truth and remind us about God.

- *Do the songs you sing in your churches teach the truth?*

For your own learning, read the rest of Moses' song in v19-43 and see what more you can learn about God and his people.

⊕ MAIN POINT
Do not forget God. Do not forget you turned away from God.

➡ TEACH: Deuteronomy 32:1-18

⊙ Start

God loves songs. There are many songs in the Bible. Moses' song is a sad song, but it is important to learn. It is important that our songs teach us the truth.

This is a song about God and God's people. God is faithful. God's people are not faithful. The aim of the song is to bring life (v1-2).

Sing about what God is like
⊙ Read: *Deuteronomy 32:3-4*

These verses tell us that God is great, perfect, just, faithful, upright and like a rock. A rock is strong and reliable. God's people must sing praise to God (v3).

Sing about what God's people are like
⊙ Read: *Deuteronomy 32:5-6*

But God's people are not like God. These verses tell us that the people of Israel were corrupt (not honest), crooked (went the wrong way), foolish and unwise. God was their Father. But the people of Israel did not behave like his children. *Tell your listeners of some of the times when God's people turned away from God in the desert.*

Sing about what God did
⊙ Read: *Deuteronomy 32:7-14*

Tell your listeners the things God did for the Israelites in the desert in these verses. God protected his people. God led them, fed them and brought them to the land. God did all this for his people, even though his people turned away from him many times.

Sing about what God's people did
⊙ Read: *Deuteronomy 32:15-18*

Because God gave everything to his people, they had much to eat. They became fat. But they turned away to other gods and made sacrifices to demons. This song reminds the people how bad they are.

❗ **Apply:** This song reminds us that God's people turn away from God many times. But God never gives up. God is faithful. The story in this song is not finished in the Old Testament. The story leads to Jesus. Jesus shows us how much God loves sinful people.

This song also tells us it is important to learn, remember and sing about God and his people. Our songs must tell what is true.

- Can you use Moses' song to make your own song of what God is like and what you are like?

⬆ **Pray:** *Thank God that he is faithful and loves his people.*

◉ **STUDY: Deuteronomy 34:1-12**

39 LOOK FORWARD TO GOD'S REST

◎ Background
Moses led the people of Israel for forty years. Moses was not allowed to enter the promised land. He died on the mountains across the Jordan river.

⊙ Read verses 1-12.
Read the passage 2 or 3 times.

⊚ Notes
- **Deuteronomy 34:1.** "Nebo", Moab" and "Pisgah" are names of places outside the promised land, over the Jordan river, where Moses spoke to the people of Israel.
- **Deuteronomy 34:9.** "Filled with the spirit of wisdom" (NIV). God gave his Spirit to Joshua to lead the people.
- **Deuteronomy 34:10.** "Face to face" means God knew Moses personally, closely. No one sees God's face.

⊙ Something to work on
Why was Moses not allowed to enter the land? Read Numbers 20: 2-13, Deuteronomy 1:37, 3:25-28, 4:21, 32:48-52. All these verses tell us Moses will not enter the land.

Do you think this is just? Moses was a great leader for a long time. He did one thing wrong. But what he did wrong was very bad. Yes, it is just. Moses did not give God respect. But God was kind. He let Moses see all the promised land (v1-4).

Verses 10-12. In Deuteronomy 18:15-18, God promised a prophet like Moses in the future. When Deuteronomy 34 was written, that prophet had not come.
- *Who is the prophet like Moses who would come later?*

Jesus is the prophet like Moses. Jesus spoke God's word. Jesus did signs and wonders. Jesus taught with more authority than Moses.
- *What does this tell us about God?*

God is holy and judges sin, even the sin of great leaders like Moses.

God is faithful. God promised a prophet like Moses. Jesus was that prophet.
- *What does this say to us?*

In Hebrews 3:7-4:11, the writer warns people not to fail to enter heaven. Moses is a warning for us. We must not fail like he did.

The good news is that Moses is in heaven (Hebrews 11:25-26). He is in heaven because of God's grace in Jesus. All Christians, including leaders, need God's grace in Jesus. We must trust Jesus always. We can be sure we will enter heaven because of Jesus.

⊕ MAIN POINT
Make sure you enter God's rest.

→ TEACH: Deuteronomy 34:1-12

⊙ Start
It is sad when people do not reach their goal. Maybe a father dies before his child's wedding day. *Give examples from your place.*

- What about Moses?

Moses cannot enter the land
⊙ Read: *Deuteronomy 34:1-8*
Moses led the people of Israel for forty years from slavery in Egypt to the promised land. But he died outside the land. God let Moses see the land but he could not enter.

Remind your listeners why Moses could not enter the land, from Numbers 20:10-12. Even though Moses was a great leader and did so many good things, he failed badly.

⊙ Apply:
We must not be like Moses. Moses is a warning to us. Especially Moses is a warning to Christian leaders. We must not fail to enter heaven because of unbelief and disobedience. Some leaders may think they will be in heaven because of all the good things they do for God. Do not rely on your good works.

Moses did not enter the earthly land. But more importantly, Moses is in heaven, the true promised land. *Tell your listeners what it says in Hebrews 11:26.* God is kind. God is forgiving. God's grace, his gift of free forgiveness, brings people into heaven through Jesus. The only way to heaven is by Jesus.

A prophet like Moses
⊙ Read: *Deuteronomy 34:9-12*
God promised a prophet like Moses. The prophet would speak God's word and do signs and wonders. When Deuteronomy 34 was written, that prophet had not come. Jesus is the prophet like Moses. Jesus spoke God's word and did many signs and wonders.

God speaks to his people by his word. Moses spoke God's word. Jesus is God's word. We hear God's word in the Bible.

⊙ Apply:
God told the people of Israel to listen to Moses. In Deuteronomy 18:15, God said the people must listen to the prophet like Moses. God's people must listen to Jesus. We listen to Jesus by reading God's word.

- How much do we read God's word? How carefully do we obey it?

⊙ Pray:
Give God thanks that we can enter heaven through Jesus. Pray we may enter God's heavenly rest. Pray we will always listen carefully to God's word about Jesus.

APPENDIX: How to apply Old Testament laws today

Many chapters of Deuteronomy tell God's laws for the people of Israel (mainly chapters 12 – 26). So the law is important in Deuteronomy. We suggest how some laws apply today. Let us think in general how Old Testament laws apply for Christians. The following are the steps to think about.

1. What is the reason for each law?
When you read a law of the Old Testament, try to think: *What is the reason for the law?* Some laws may have the reason to love your neighbour. Some are about worshipping only God. Some are because the people of Israel must be different from other nations. Some laws are about safety. Some are about fair justice. Some protect the poor.

Many of the Old Testament laws are examples. A person must help their neighbour's ox or donkey (Deuteronomy 22:4). What about the neighbour's sheep? Of course the law would apply for a sheep too. In this example, we know the reason for the law is care for our neighbour's animals. So the law applies for other animals too.

It is not always easy to find the reason for a law. What is the reason for the law that you shall not boil a young goat in its mother's milk? It is hard for us to know. But probably the reason is to stop the people of Israel following the behaviour of people of other religions.

2. Most reasons still apply today.
Most of the reasons for the laws still apply. The New Testament does not change many reasons for the laws. Christians should love their neighbour, worship only God, have safe places, be fair and just, and be different from unbelievers. Many laws still apply for Christians. God's standards of love and holiness have not changed.

3. Some reasons apply but our culture is different.
Many of us live in different cultures from ancient Israel. One example is houses. In Old Testament times, people had flat roofs on their houses. For safety, they must make a parapet or fence on the roof (Deuteronomy 22:8). Many cultures do not have flat roofs. This law about fences does not apply. But the reason of safety still applies. There are other ways we must make our house safe. For example, to make the electric wires safe or make the cooking place safe for children.

4. Some reasons change because Jesus fulfils laws.

Jesus fulfils the sacrifices of the Old Testament. Christians must not offer animal sacrifices. Christians are right with God only because they trust in the sacrifice of Jesus on the cross for our sin. The sacrifices of the Old Testament point to Jesus' sacrifice on the cross. Jesus' sacrifice is the true and only sacrifice for believers today (Hebrews 10:11-12). Also Jesus is the living temple (John 2:21). Christians do not go to a tabernacle or temple or Jerusalem to worship God. Christians go to Jesus to worship God. There is no special place for worship any more. Christians apply the Old Testament laws about sacrifice and temple through Jesus.

Also Jesus expands the principles. Christians must also love their enemies. Christians must not hate or lust.

5. Some reasons change because God's people now are not one nation.

God's people are now a church in every nation. The worldwide church is the fulfilment of the nation of ancient Israel. Some reasons for Old Testament laws are based on God's people as a nation. So the reason for the Old Testament laws about the nation changed. One example: In Deuteronomy, an Israelite who has wrong sexual relations is put to death. Now, a Christian who has wrong sexual relations may be sent out of the church (1 Corinthians 5:1-5). Old Testament laws about the nation need to be applied to the church of God's people.

6. Some reasons change because the kingdom of heaven replaces the earthly promised land.

Christians do not have to live in the earthly promised land like ancient Israel. The land that is important is the heavenly land. So the law about conquering the land does not apply to Christians. Christians fight a spiritual battle to make sure they arrive in heaven. Jesus has defeated our main enemy, Satan, on the cross. Christians can be sure of victory because of Jesus.

7. Some reasons change because God's people now are Jews and Gentiles.

In the Old Testament, foreigners are treated as different from the people of God. The Israelites must behave different from foreigners. For example, the food laws in Deuteronomy 14 show this. When Jesus came, the good news of sins forgiven is for Gentiles and Jews. So all foods are made clean in Acts 10. Now Jewish and Gentile Christians are not different because of Christ.

8. Why we Obey God.

We must remember the reason why we obey God's laws. The people of Israel were to fear and obey God because he rescued them from Egypt. Christians are to trust and obey God because he rescues us on the cross. Only in Jesus are we saved. Israelites and Christians must not rely on obeying all God's law. God wants faith seen in obedience from his people in Old and New Testaments. Believers are not saved by keeping the law. Believers are saved by Christ alone through faith. That faith is seen in obedience. We must live a life worthy of Jesus (Ephesians 4:1).

9. Summary.

So look for the reason behind the Old Testament law. Think if anything has changed from then to now. Has anything changed because of Jesus? What difference is made to that law? Think how it applies to your life. Then follow in faith! When you are not sure, pray and find a wise Christian to help guide you.

E: LESSONS FROM DEUTERONOMY

It is important to take lessons from God's word into our lives. It will help your people to discuss these questions in groups and pray about them. The questions help us to learn some of the main lessons from this book. You can use these questions after you have finished all your talks on Deuteronomy. Or you may want to use them after each section.

1. Deuteronomy 1:1-8
- What is Deuteronomy about? Why do we need to be reminded of God's word?
- What is important about the promised land (verse 8)?

2. Deuteronomy 1:9-18
- Look at God's promises in verses 10-11. What promises of God do you have trouble trusting?
- What type of people should be church leaders (verses 15-18)?

3. Deuteronomy 1:19-33
- Look at verse 28. Think about what you fear. Why do you fear these things
- Now look at verses 32-33. When you disobey God, is it because you do not trust him?

4. Deuteronomy 1:34-46
- Moses and the adult Israelites did not enter the promised land. Caleb and Joshua did because they trusted and obeyed (verses 34-38). How do you make

every effort to enter the heavenly promised land? Consider Hebrews 4:11.
- How does the action of the people of Israel show they do not really repent (verses 41-45)?

5. Deuteronomy 2:1 – 3:11
- What enemies are you afraid of? How is God able to protect you from those enemies?
- God is God over the nations. How does this give you hope in the world today?

6. Deuteronomy 3:23-29
- How do you pray for your church leaders that they do not fall into sin?
- If you are a leader of God's people, how do you make sure you keep obeying God?

7. Deuteronomy 4:1-8
- Look at verse 4. How do you hold fast / stay faithful to the Lord?
- Look again at verses 6-8. Have you seen unbelievers coming to God because of the obedience of Christians?

8. Deuteronomy 4:9-20
- Look at verse 9. What do you do so that you do not forget what God has said and done?
- Look at what verses 15-16 say about idols. What idols are common in your place? How do you make sure you do not worship idols or false gods?

9. Deuteronomy 4:21-31
- Look at verse 24. What does it mean in your life that God is a jealous God?
- Look at verse 31. What does it mean in your life that God is a merciful God?

10. Deuteronomy 4:32-40
- How is the God of the Bible greater than the gods of other people in your place?
- When you are speaking to a worshipper of other gods, how would you compare their gods to the God of the Bible?

11. Deuteronomy 5:6-11
- Look at the commandment in verse 7. What other gods do Christians in your place sometimes worship as well as the real God?
- Look at verses 8-9. What idols are temptations in your place?

12. Deuteronomy 5:12-15
- How do you rest each week?
- Look at verse 15. How do you remember what God has done to give you rest?

13. Deuteronomy 5:16-21
- Look at verse 17. Remember Jesus said that we break this commandment by being angry with people (Matthew 5:21-22). Who are you angry with?
- Look at verse 18. Jesus said we commit adultery by looking at someone with lust (Matthew 5:28). What lustful thoughts do you need to stop?

14. Deuteronomy 6:4-9
- Look at verse 5. If you were able to measure how much you loved God, out of 100, what would the score be?
- Now look at verse 6. How do you try to get God's words into your heart?

15. Deuteronomy 6:20-25
- If a child asks you why they must obey God, how would you answer?
- How well does your church teach your children about God?

16. Deuteronomy 7:1-11
- Look at verse 6. How different is your life from unbelievers in your place? Can other people see that you are holy and belong to God?
- Look at verse 8. Does it make a difference to you to remember that God loves you?

17. Deuteronomy 8:1-20
- What lessons have you learned from hard times in your life?
- Look at verses 17-18. What dangers are there in your place for becoming rich?

18. Deuteronomy 9:4-24
- Do you ever think that you are better than other people? Do you think this is why God has blessed you (verses 4-6)?
- Look at verse 12. Can you remember times when you were quick to turn away from God?

19. Deuteronomy 9:25-29
- How do you pray for people in church who do bad things and maybe give up the faith?
- How can you pray for your church to do the right thing so unbelievers will see how you live, and so come to God?

20. Deuteronomy 10:12-22
- Look at verse 16. How does this happen? Is your heart circumcised?
- Look at verses 21-22. Is God your praise? How do you praise God each day?

21. Deuteronomy 12:1-7
- Look at verse 5. What is the centre of your worship of God? (See John 2:21)
- Look at verse 7. Is your worship of God joyful? In what ways is it joyful?

22. Deuteronomy 13:1-11
- Do you have false prophets in your place? How do you warn your people against them?
- Look at verses 1-4. Do people in your place follow others who do miracles or make predictions?

23. Deuteronomy 14:1-21
- Are people in your place invited to share in pagan meals? How do you advise them what to do?
- In what ways do Christians in your place still do things the unbelievers do?

24. Deuteronomy 14:22-29
- How do you decide what to give to Christian ministry and mission?
- How does your giving teach you to trust God (verse 23)?

25. Deuteronomy 15:1-18
- Does your church have ways of helping poor Christians with loans of money?
- How does your church share possessions to help poor Christians?

26. Deuteronomy 16:1-17
- How do you celebrate the important Christian festivals, such as Christmas and Easter?
- Do you celebrate them in ways that help believers remember what God has done?
- Do you often celebrate with joy what God has done?

27. Deuteronomy 17:14-20
- Think about the warnings for the king: horses, wives and riches. Money, sex and power are common temptations. How do you resist these temptations?

- Are these temptations worse for leaders?

28. Read Deuteronomy 18:9-19
- Look at verses 9-11. What diviners or witchdoctors or people like that are in your place?
- How are they a danger for believers where you are?
- Look at verse 15. The prophet like Moses is Jesus. How do you listen to Jesus?

29. Deuteronomy 22:1-12
- Look at verses 1-4. How can believers care better for each other's possessions?
- Look at verse 8. Discuss ideas about making your house and property safer for people.

30. Deuteronomy 22:13-30
- Why do people often fall into sexual sin?
- How can the church help and strengthen Christians to be faithful in marriage?

31. Deuteronomy 26:1-11
- What has the Lord done for you? Write something like verses 5-10 for your life.
- What are the good things God has given you? Also read Ephesians 1:3-14.

32. Deuteronomy 27:1-13
- How does Jesus fulfil Old Testament law?
- When you read the Old Testament law, does it make you see your sin and failure?
- Read Galatians 3:10-14. Do you always have joy for forgiveness from sin and freedom from the law? Praise God.

33. Deuteronomy 28:1-14
- Look at verse 10. If ancient Israel obeyed God and was blessed, what should other nations and peoples think?
- What blessings has God has given you?
- Read Ephesians 1:3-14. Are unbelievers coming to God through your church?

34. Deuteronomy 28:15-68
- What is the reason why God will curse someone?
- What has Jesus done to take the curse for us?

35. Deuteronomy 30:1-10
- Look at verse 6. Has God changed your heart? How do you know this?
- Look at verses 1-3. Have you turned back to God? What do you need to do?

36. Deuteronomy 30:11-20
- Look at verse 19. What does it mean to choose life?
- How important is the theme of life in the words and life of Jesus?

37. Deuteronomy 31:1-13
- Look at verse 7. What gives you courage and confidence?
- Look at verse 13. How often do you and your children hear God's word together?

38. Deuteronomy 32:1-18
- How has verse 4 been true in your life?
- Look at verse 18. Why do people desert/forget God, the Rock who gives them life?

39. Deuteronomy 34:1-12
- Look at verse 9. Why is wisdom important for the leaders of God's people?
- Look at verse 10. How is Jesus a prophet like Moses?

Opening up the Bible

At The Good Book Company, we are dedicated to helping Christians and local churches grow. We believe that God's growth process always starts with hearing clearly what he has said to us through his timeless word—the Bible.

Ever since we opened our doors in 1991, we have been striving to produce resources that honour God in the way the Bible is used. We have grown to become an international provider of user-friendly resources to the Christian community, with believers of all backgrounds and denominations using our Bible studies, books, evangelistic resources, DVD-based courses and training events.

We want to equip ordinary Christians to live for Christ day by day, and churches to grow in their knowledge of God, their love for one another, and the effectiveness of their outreach.

Call us for a discussion of your needs or visit one of our local websites for more information on the resources and services we provide.

UK & Europe: www.thegoodbook.co.uk
North America: www.thegoodbook.com
Australia: www.thegoodbook.com.au
New Zealand: www.thegoodbook.co.nz

UK & Europe: 0333 123 0880
North America: 866 244 2165
Australia: (02) 6100 4211
New Zealand (+64) 3 343 1990

www.christianityexplored.org

Our partner site is a great place for those exploring the Christian faith, with a clear explanation of the good news, powerful testimonies and answers to difficult questions.

One life. What's it all about?